W9-BTG-128

R. B. Cunninghame Graham

Twayne's English Authors Series

Herbert Sussman, Editor

Northeastern University

TEAS 357

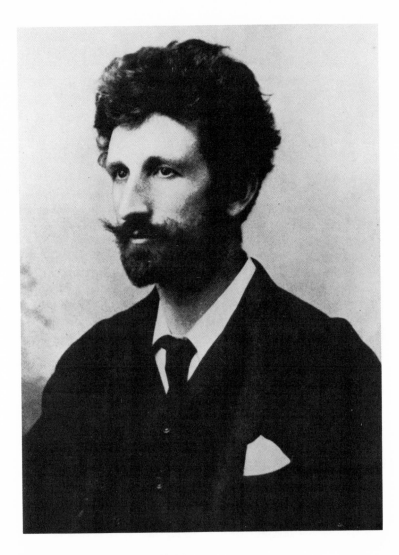

R. B. CUNNINGHAME GRAHAM
(1852–1936)

R. B. Cunninghame Graham

By Cedric Watts

University of Sussex

Twayne Publishers • Boston

R. B. Cunninghame Graham

Cedric Watts

#9016728

Copyright © 1983 by G. K. Hall & Company
All Rights Reserved
Published by Twayne Publishers
A Division of G. K. Hall & Company
70 Lincoln Street
Boston, Massachusetts 02111

Book Production by Marne B. Sultz
Book Design by Barbara Anderson

Printed on permanent/durable acid-free
paper and bound in The United States of
America.

Library of Congress Cataloging in Publication Data

Watts, Cedric Thomas.
    R. B. Cunninghame Graham.

    (Twayne's English authors series ; TEAS 357)
    Bibliography: p. 124
    Includes index.
    1. Cunninghame Graham, R. B. (Robert Bontine),
1856–1936—Criticism and interpretation.
I. Title. II. Series.
PR6013.R19Z883   1983   828'.91209   82–21330
ISBN 0–8057–6843–2

Contents

About the Author
Preface and Acknowledgments
Abbreviations
Chronology

Chapter One
Biographical   1

Chapter Two
Earliest Writings   34

Chapter Three
The Histories   68

Chapter Four
Tales and Essays of His Middle Period   82

Chapter Five
The Biographies   99

Chapter Six
The Later Collections   106

Chapter Seven
Conclusion   114

Notes and References   119
Selected Bibliography   124
Index   128

About the Author

Cedric Watts was born at Cheltenham in 1937. After serving in the Royal Navy, he read English at Cambridge University, graduating with a First in 1961 and subsequently taking a doctorate. Since 1965 he has taught in the School of English and American Studies at the University of Sussex. He is author of *Conrad's "Heart of Darkness": A Critical and Contextual Discussion* (1977) and *A Preface to Conrad* (1982), and coauthor with Laurence Davies of *Cunninghame Graham: A Critical Biography* (1979). He has edited *Joseph Conrad's Letters to R. B. Cunninghame Graham* (1969), *The English Novel* (1976), and *Selected Writings of Cunninghame Graham* (1981). His articles on Shakespeare, Ibsen, Beckett, and others have appeared in various books and periodicals.

Preface and Acknowledgments

Cunninghame Graham's literary career began around 1890; his subsequent output was huge, and much of it was very highly regarded in his lifetime. Yet this book is the first commercially published volume devoted to the critical assessment of Graham the writer. In addition, substantial numbers of his tales and essays have recently been republished in several volumes of selections. So there are grounds for thinking that after the intervening years of neglect, there may now be some regrowth of interest in this strange and vivid author. If so, the world may become a slightly better place, for he was a shrewd and humane observer of life; if not, the loss will be ours.

Cunninghame Graham was not a major writer (though in his time he was a major character), but to classify him as one of the many minor authors of that period does injustice to his distinctiveness and to his numerous successes in the generically ambiguous territory of the short "sketch" and in autobiographical travel-writing. Furthermore, even the worst parts of his output—the slighter ruminations, the patchier histories of the Spanish Conquest—through their themes and preoccupations contribute to a complicated pattern which has an interesting logic and integrity: for we enter the complex and oblique autobiography of a man whose life was a conscious project—a career that was adventurous, protean, colorful, and paradoxical.

He himself has said:

I believe that, be it bad or good, all that a writer does is to dress up what he has seen, or felt, or heard, and nothing real is evolved from his own brain, except the words he uses, and the way in which he uses them. Therefore it follows, that in writing he sets down (perhaps unwittingly) the story of his life, and as he does so, makes it worth reading only by chronicling all his impressions of the world quite honestly, as if he were alone upon a desert island (as in fact he is) and he were writing on the sand. (*His People*, x)

He was defending his chief limitation or control: the adherence to what he had experienced and his reluctance to move freely into the territory of fiction. The winds of time have not yet entirely obliterated his writings on the sand, and the story that they combine to tell is eloquent enough.

In the subsequent chapters, I first make a biographical survey and next discuss, in chronological order as far as is convenient, a large selection of his shorter pieces and virtually all his books of travel, history, and biography. (Anyone who wishes to seek out his minor, uncollected items of journalism may consult my list of approximately 400 contributions that he made to periodicals: see *The Bibliotheck,* Glasgow, 4 [1965]: 186–99.) Inevitably, I have drawn on some of my previous commentaries on Cunninghame Graham, in *Joseph Conrad's Letters to R. B. Cunninghame Graham* and in the biography (*Cunninghame Graham: A Critical Biography*) which I wrote with Dr. Laurence Davies; but such commentaries have been reconsidered in the light of further readings of the texts. To Dr. Davies, my friend and colleague, I owe a long-standing debt for ideas acquired during our work on Cunninghame Graham at Sussex University and thereafter.

When, just now, I referred to this book as the first "commercially published" study of Cunninghame Graham the writer, I used that phrase to imply the prior existence of a privately published study: Richard E. Haymaker's *Prince-Errant and Evocator of Horizons: A Reading of R. B. Cunninghame Graham,* 1967, which offers a richly detailed discussion. I have enjoyed comparing views with Haymaker, and I hope his book becomes more widely known. As before, I gratefully acknowledge the hospitality and assistance given to me over many years by Cunninghame Graham's family: particularly by his nephew, Admiral Sir Angus Cunninghame Graham, K.B.E., C.B., and his great-niece, Lady Polwarth. Since I began my researches in 1961, they have been unfailingly cooperative.

For permission to quote the writings of R. B. Cunninghame Graham, I am grateful to his literary executors, Lady Polwarth and Mr. Andrew Hewson. For permission to quote the letter from H. G. Wells, I thank Professor G. P. Wells. The Society of Authors on behalf of the Bernard Shaw Estate allowed me to quote the writings of George Bernard Shaw. Dr. Laurence Davies kindly permitted me to quote his unpublished D.Phil. thesis, "Cunninghame

Preface and Acknowledgments

Graham and the Concept of Impressionism." The frontispiece is by courtesy of Graham's literary executors.

In quotations, an editorial omission is indicated by a row of five dots (. . . . .), while a row of three dots indicates an ellipsis already present in the cited text. When quoting Graham's writings, I have, apart from such editorial omissions and the insertion of a few clarifications in square brackets, preserved the original text without correction or alteration. (Thus, on page 14, for example, I have not changed "massacre." to "massacre?", nor, on page 42, have I changed "Pulperia" to "pulpería".) His work contains many petty errors; to preserve them is to preserve a reminder of the recklessness which was part of his charcter.

Cedric Watts

Abbreviations

AFT A. F. Tschiffely: *Don Roberto*. London: Heinemann, 1937.

BF R. B. Cunninghame Graham: *Brought Forward*. London: Duckworth, 1916.

FA G. and R. B. Cunninghame Graham: *Father Archangel of Scotland, and Other Essays*. London: Black, 1896.

Graham R. B. Cunninghame Graham.

H R. B. Cunninghame Graham: *A Hatchment*. London: Duckworth, 1913.

HFW H. F. West: *A Modern Conquistador: Robert Bontine Cunninghame Graham: His Life and Works*. London: Cranley and Day, 1932.

IK R. B. Cunninghame Graham: *The Imperial Kailyard, Being a Biting Satire on English Colonisation*. London: Twentieth Century Press, 1896.

IP R. B. Cunninghame Graham: *The Ipané*. London: Fisher Unwin, 1899.

JCL Cedric T. Watts, ed.: *Joseph Conrad's Letters to R. B. Cunninghame Graham*. London: Cambridge, 1969.

LD Laurence Davies: "R. B. Cunninghame Graham and the Concept of Impressionism." University of Sussex D.Phil. thesis, 1972.

M R. B. Cunninghame Graham: *Mogreb-el-Acksa: A Journey in Morocco*. London: Heinemann, 1898.

ND R. B. Cunninghame Graham: *Notes on the District of Menteith, for Tourists and Others*. London: Black, 1895.

NLS The National Library of Scotland, Edinburgh.

PC The manuscript collection of Lady Polwarth.

PD R. B. Cunninghame Graham: *Portrait of a Dictator: Francisco Solano López (Paraguay 1865–1870)*. London: Heinemann, 1933.

PP *The People's Press* (London).

R. B. CUNNINGHAME GRAHAM

RH Richard E. Haymaker: *Prince-Errant and Evocator of Horizons: A Reading of R. B. Cunninghame Graham.* Kingsport, Tenn.: privately printed, 1967.

SR *Saturday Review* (London).

TS R. B. Cunninghame Graham: *Thirteen Stories.* London: Heinemann, 1900.

VA R. B. Cunninghame Graham: *A Vanished Arcadia: Being Some Account of the Jesuits in Paraguay, 1607–1767.* London, Heinemann, 1901.

WD Cedric Watts and Laurence Davies: *Cunninghame Graham: A Critical Biography.* London: Cambridge University Press, 1979.

Chronology

1852   Robert Bontine Cunninghame Graham born in London, 24 May.

1865–1867   At Harrow School.

1868   Education continues at Brussels.

1870   Aged seventeen, Robert sets out for Argentina; until late 1871 travels and works there as cattle-rancher and horse-dealer.

1873–1874   In Paraguay, Robert works as surveyor and negotiator in the *mate* (Paraguayan tea) trade.

1876–1877   With G. M. Mansel, ranching and horse-dealing in Uruguay, Brazil, and Argentina.

1878   Marries Gabriela (Gabrielle de la Balmondière) at a London Registry Office.

1879–1881   To New Orleans with Gabriela; travels in Texas and Mexico.

1883   Father dies; Robert inherits large Scottish estates.

1886–1892   Elected to Parliament as Liberal, but soon proves to be the first Socialist M.P. Condemns capitalism, imperialism, and racial intolerance; advocates nationalization of industry, free education, eight-hour working day, and Home Rule for Ireland and Scotland. Outside Parliament, campaigns with William Morris, H. M. Hyndman, and Keir Hardie.

1887   "Bloody Sunday": Graham arrested at the Battle of Trafalgar Square (13 November).

1888   Sentenced to six weeks' imprisonment at Pentonville Jail. Founds Scottish Labour Party (the first Labour Party in Great Britain).

1889   Campaigns with John Burns, Prince Kropotkin, and Ben Tillett for the London dockers.

1890   Campaigns with Friedrich Engels, Stepniak, and G. B. Shaw for eight-hour working day. Attends Marxist Congress at Paris with William Morris and Edward Carpenter.

1891   Arrested and expelled from France after speech denouncing the authorities.

1892   Stands as Labour candidate at election; defeated.

1894   Robert and Gabriela prospect for gold in Spain.

1895   His first book published: *Notes on the District of Menteith*.

1895–1905   Friendships with Conrad, Hudson, Blunt, Garnett, Lavery, and Rothenstein; meets and corresponds with Henry James, Wilde, Hardy, Wells, Martin Hume, and Roger Casement. Writes for Frank Harris's *Saturday Review* in company of Wells, Shaw, Symons, and Winston Churchill. Helps Shaw with *Captain Brassbound's Conversion* and Conrad with *Nostromo*.

1897   Travels in Morocco disguised as an Arab; held captive by Kaid of Kintafi.

1898   *Mogreb-el-Acksa*.

1899   *The Ipané*.

1900   *Thirteen Stories*. Graham auctions Gartmore, his ancestral home.

1901   *A Vanished Arcadia*.

1902   *Success*.

1903   *Hernando de Soto*.

1905   *Progress*.

1906   *His People*. Gabriela dies in France.

1909   *Faith*.

1910   *Hope*.

1910–1913   Widespread social and industrial unrest in Great Britain; Graham campaigns for militant socialism with Hyndman, Tillett, Victor Grayson, and Jim Larkin.

1912   *Charity*.

1913   *A Hatchment*.

1914 Graham first opposes the war, then gains employment at War Office: travels to South America to buy horses for the troops.

1915 *Bernal Díaz del Castillo.*

1916 *Brought Forward.*

1916–1917 Surveys cattle resources of Colombia for British Government.

1918 Seeks election as Liberal M.P.: defeated.

1918–1936 Leader of Scottish Nationalists; associated with Eric Linklater, Compton Mackenzie, and Hugh Mac-Diarmid.

1920 *A Brazilian Mystic; Cartagena and the Banks of the Sinú.*

1922 *The Conquest of New Granada.* Death of Blunt and Hudson.

1924 *The Conquest of the River Plate.* Death of Conrad.

1925 *Doughty Deeds.* Death of his mother, Mrs. Bontine.

1925 *Pedro de Valdivia.*

1927 *Redeemed.*

1929 *José Antonio Páez.*

1930 *The Horses of the Conquest.*

1932 *Writ in Sand.* Biography by H. F. West, *A Modern Conquistador.*

1933 *Portrait of a Dictator.*

1936 *Mirages.* Graham dies in Argentina (20 March) and is later buried on Inchmahome in the Scottish Lake of Menteith.

Chapter One
Biographical

Retrospect

One class of writers is the class of notable has-beens. In their day these writers were famous or prestigious; subsequently they have become neglected and forgotten; and from time to time attempts are made by commentators to revive their reputations, but the authors resist revival: they simply have not been good enough to last, it seems. R. B. Cunninghame Graham may be one of these, but there are some grounds for thinking that his destiny may be more fortunate. He was indeed famous—variously illustrious and notorious—in his lifetime, and prestigious as "a writer's writer"; subsequently he has indeed been neglected and generally forgotten; but the intermittent "rediscoveries" have been rather more frequent in recent years, and there may at last be adequate recognition of Cunninghame Graham's masterpiece.

That masterpiece, as his contemporaries recognized, was himself, in all his vividness and paradoxical variety. Let us remind ourselves of those contemporary opinions. Here is Jacob Epstein, the sculptor: "Imagine Don Quixote walking about your studio and sitting for his portrait! This was R. B. Cunninghame Graham. . . . . ." Here is another admirer, Arthur Symons, the poet and influential critic: "A dreamer with a passion for action, one whose dreams are action, yet whose actions are certainly for the most part dreams, Cunninghame Graham brings a touch of the Elizabethan spirit into contemporary life, urgent, unpractical, haughty, at war with the world, yet loving the world for its own sake." George Bernard Shaw, in the course of a brilliantly flattering pen-portrait, said that he had refrained from making Graham the hero of one of his plays "because so incredible a personage must have destroyed its likelihood—such as it is. There are moments when I do not myself believe in his existence. And yet he must be real; for I have seen him with these

eyes. . . . ." G. K. Chesterton asserted: "Nothing could prevent
Balfour being Prime Minister or MacDonald being Prime Minister;
but Cunninghame Graham achieved the adventure of being Cunninghame Graham. . . . . It is an achievement so fantastic that
it would never be believed in romance." And the painter John
Lavery, whose work Graham had helped to promote, said of him:

Some people complain that he remained an amateur and playboy. But he
was not an amateur in his own art, the art of personality. That art is rare
and calls for great devotion and labour. It has few masters. . . . . Graham's job was to create himself, he had the material. It was unnecessary
for him to do more, like T. E. Lawrence (for whom he had great admiration,
seeing in him a superb Irish playboy). But the latter had no personality—
so he had to take Arabia.

I think I did something to help Graham in the creation of his masterpiece—himself. [1]

Some of these judgments may be influenced by the tastes of the
1890s, the era of Aestheticism, when paradoxes, large and small,
were in fashion, and when it was also fashionable to claim that life
imitated art (just as London's brown fogs, in Wilde's view, obviously
flowed from Impressionist canvases). Fifty years later, the existen-
tialists were to argue that one's personality should be deliberately
constructed, like an artefact. If a masterpiece is original, forceful,
colorful, complex, and challenging, Lavery's claim that Cunninghame Graham constituted one is fully justified. As Epstein has
reminded us, Graham was known as "Don Roberto" and "The
Modern Don Quixote" because of his Spanish ancestry and appearance and because of his questing, bold, and impetuous life-style.
To students of the intricacies of Scottish history he was also "The
Uncrowned King of Scotland," because of his aristocratic descent
from Robert the Bruce, King Robert I, who had once walked the
leafy paths of the ancestral island where the later Robert is now
buried.

Cunninghame Graham had several careers: one was as traveler,
adventurer, and fortune-seeker in various parts of the world—Argentina, Paraguay, Uruguay, Texas, Mexico, Spain, Morocco. In
politics, he gained notoriety as demagogue and controversialist, a
radical campaigning figure who was jailed during his time as a
parliamentarian and was expelled from France for making an in-
flammatory speech. He was a political columnist, literary essayist,

critic, historian, biographer, translator, and story-writer. As a picturesque social celebrity he moved among the worlds of factory girls,
courtesans, circus performers, artists, scholars, editors: he knew
Buffalo Bill and Henry James, Engels and Conrad, Keir Hardie and
Whistler. Although he was a prolific and respected writer, he was
also a celebrated equestrian, an able swordsman, and "a first-class
shot with pistols" who retained his agility and stamina into old age,
climbing trees and leaping streams like a silver-haired boy.

Laurence Davies indicates some of the paradoxes of the man:
"Graham was a socialist who went regularly to the Eton and Harrow
cricket match; an asthmatic who slept out on the Venezuelan *llanos*
in his seventies; a solitary who seems to have known half London;
an internationalist who preached nationalism; an anti-clerical who
fell easily into theological language, used to quote the Bible, and
defended the Jesuits; a landlord who advocated nationalisation of
the land; a J.P. [Justice of the Peace] and Deputy Lieutenant jailed
for unlawful assembly . . ." (*LD,* 16).

He was handsome and vain, walking with the proud swagger of
a Spanish grandee; he was bold and impetuous; yet he was com-
passionate and kindly, with a keenly sympathetic eye for the underdogs of the world, whether they were starving workers, shivering
hobos, or the black victims of white oppression. He was so adventurous and picturesque that sometimes he seems to inhabit a unique
territory: Grahamland, a region where fact and fiction, reality and
fantasy, blend into one another. Some of his adventures sound like
romantic fiction but prove to be hard fact; others ascribed to him
purport to be fact but prove to be fiction; some of his tales seem
like fiction but prove to be accurate autobiography. Slim, wiry, and
erect, rufous-haired and sharp-eyed, he moves in and out of the art
and literature of his period: for example, he was the model for
Simeon Solomon's painting of Sir Walter Raleigh and for some of
William Strang's etchings illustrating *Don Quixote,* and he appears
in various guises in the pages of Conrad, Shaw, and Galsworthy.
In a novel by Vernon Lee, a character says of a seventeenth-century
ancestor: "I always thought that if Louis Norbert had lived in our
day he would have been a sort of Cunninghame Graham (how awfully
good those last stories of his are!) and held pro-Ferrer meetings in
Trafalgar Square, and ridden a mustang and gone to prison for his
opinions, and all the time dreadfully an aristocrat and hating publicity."[2] H. G. Wells, who mentions Graham in *Boon* and *Tono-*

Bungay, wrote to him in 1902: "I'd like to bandy argument tremendous. When will you be along? Then we can arrange for clean sawdust in the arena. . . . . You know I know nothing about Arabic & Spanish & I want to. And if you know any way of being steadily & permanently happy without fixing on to some ampler issue than the immediate present I'll be glad of the *recipe.*"[3] Graham was mobile stimulus to an age. He was mythogenic: a generator and attractor of legends; a challenge to the artistic imagination. As Henry James confided to him: "I like making an impression on a man who is constantly seeing, as I imagine, far & strange & thrilling things—beyond any the likes of my so little adventurous muse can figure; & who still, though he might be so blasé, remains accessible to my mild magic" (*JCL,* 47).

As all these quotations help to establish, Cunninghame Graham—traveler, adventurer, political extremist, and "writer's writer" praised by Conrad, Shaw, Galsworthy, and Ford—enjoyed half a century of fame. By 1888, when he was thirty-five, he was a public celebrity, reported, interviewed, and caricatured in newspapers and magazines, a figure hero-worshiped by some, scorned by others; seen as a mixture of eccentric, dandy, maverick, nobleman, cavalier, revolutionary, aesthete, firebrand, humanitarian, and cynic. When he wrote to Joseph Conrad in 1897 to praise "An Outpost of Progress," Conrad's response tells us which of the two was then the famous figure: "You've given me a few moments of real, solid excitement. I scuttled about for the signature—then laid the letter down. I am a prudent man. Very soon it occurred to me that you would hardly go out of your way (in the month of August) to kick an utter stranger. So, I said to myself 'These—no doubt—are halfpence. Let us see' and—behold! it was real gold, a ducat for a beggar—a treasure for the very poor!" (*JCL,* 45). In 1913 the glamour of the man was well shown by Ford Madox Hueffer's dedication of the novel *Mr. Fleight* "To that Unsurpassed Writer of English, / Unveiler of Mogreb el Acksa / and Chronicler of the Conquistadores / R. B. CUNNINGHAME GRAHAM / of Right King of Scotland, / Known to this Dully Revolving World as a Revolutionist / and in All Realms of Adventure / Most Chivalrous."

Cunninghame Graham became a celebrity abroad as well as in Britain. When he died in 1936 on a visit to Argentina, the land which he had so often recalled in his tales, the immense procession of mourners filled the streets; the funeral oration was spoken by the

British ambassador, and the President of the Republic came to pay his respects. And the fame crossed frontiers between classes as well as between nations: at home he was mourned by many who remembered his early struggles for the rights of the workers in the heroic era of the labor movement, and among those at the memorial service in London was John Burns, the former engineer and revolutionary who had once been jailed with Cunninghame Graham in the aftermath of Bloody Sunday.

After Graham's death, the slow oblivion beset his public reputation. The first biography of him had appeared in 1932 and the second came in 1937; but then over forty years were to elapse before a new biography appeared. His books were seldom reprinted, and gathered dust on the shelves. (When, in 1962, I asked a secondhand book-seller if he had anything by Cunninghame Graham, he remarked that as I was the first person ever to make that request, my taste deserved its reward; and he searched out and presented me with a first edition of *The Ipané.*) In studies of the literature or the politics of his period, Graham was often ignored or relegated to a passing (and not always accurate) reference.

By this relative neglect, a major irony was generated. All his life, Cunninghame Graham was preoccupied by death and oblivion—by the fact that the vivid moments of the past fade from our memories, friends go their separate ways, and acts of nobility are forgotten. By his writings, he strove again and again to give historic immortality—immortality in the imaginations of men—to the sights and places, the incidents and people, that he had encountered in his many journeyings. It is, then, a poignant yet appropriate irony that in the four decades after his death, his numerous achievements in politics and literature and in sheer selfhood should have faded almost completely from public memory. If we retrace his career now, we may reduce the injustice by recalling some of those achievements.

The Protean Life

Early Years. Robert Bontine Cunninghame Graham was born at 5 Cadogan Place in London on 25 May 1852, in the fifteenth year of Queen Victoria's reign. It was a hard birth: his father gave the laboring mother chloroform to dull her pangs, as he told a relative later that day. "Thank God it is well over. A young gentleman appeared at one o'clock this Morning (Monday). Poor Missy is doing very well but has had a dreadfully severe trial. I had to give her chloroform for nearly an hour . . . . . for some time her case appeared very serious. She has suffered a great deal poor child. . . . ."[4] Robert, who to his father resembled a dark-eyed tadpole, was thus born into the Scottish landowning gentry; for although the family had bases in London, Leamington, and the Isle of Wight, its great estates were in Scotland. The family's surnames were signs of its possessions. There had long been "the Grahams of Gartmore"; and on inheriting the estate of Ardoch from the Bontine family in the eighteenth century, the Grahams had agreed to keep the name Bontine alive by alternating it with their own. The name Cunninghame came with the further estate, Finlaystone, on the south banks of the Clyde. So Robert's father was known as William Bontine, and Robert himself was "Cunninghame Graham Bontine" until his father's death, upon which the "Bontine" was shuffled into a subordinate position.

In addition to over a thousand acres of land around Ardoch, near Dumbarton, the family owned that vast estate, covering hundreds of square miles of beautiful moorland, woodland, and hillside, at Gartmore in Perthshire. The family was quite literally a *feudal* family, for the basis of its wealth was the income provided by the *feu*-duties—the fees and rents—paid by the hundreds of farmers, cottagers, and other tenants who lived and worked on the Grahams' lands. At the heart of the estate was the family's ancestral home: the great house called Gartmore, an imposing château-like mansion whose tall windows looked out over the ballustraded terraces toward the wild peaty moors and the rolling hills dominated by Ben Lomond. Nearby, in the Lake of Menteith, is the island, Inchmahome, with its ruined Augustinian priory where once the young Queen Mary stayed. The Queen of Scots had taken sanctuary there after the Battle of Pinkie in 1547.

The Christian name "Robert" was a reminder that the Graham family could trace its ancestry back to another visitor to that sheltered leafy island—Robert the Bruce, King Robert I of Scotland (1274–1329); indeed, some commentators would suggest that Robert Bontine Cunninghame Graham was "The Uncrowned King of Scotland": the true heir to the Scottish, and therefore (as the Scottish royal line had provided British monarchs) to the British throne. The story, somewhat shrouded by the mists of antiquity, was this. The first of the Stewart or Stuart kings, Robert II, had had numerous illegitimate children by a mistress, Elizabeth, whom he eventually had married. Subsequently, he had legitimate children by a second wife, Euphemia. After his death, the next monarch was Robert III, the eldest son of Elizabeth; but as this successor had been born out of wedlock, some Scots believed that the throne should really have been the heritage of the descendants of Euphemia—the Grahams: hence the family tradition that their blood was "redder than the king's."

In any case, the Grahams were claimants to the Earldoms of Menteith, Strathearn, and Airth (the Earldom of Menteith having been created to reward one of the vanquishers of Macbeth, according to Holinshed's *Chronicles*); and the family's history was amply picturesque. One ancestor was Sir John Grahame of the Bright Sword, who was slain at Falkirk in 1298 while fighting alongside William Wallace, Scotland's greatest national hero, against the English. Another was Sir Robert Grahame, who hunted down and murdered the Scottish King James I. Family tradition held that Nicol Graham of Gartmore had defied the extortionate Rob Roy MacGregor and actually held him captive; Sir Walter Scott's novel *Rob Roy* drew on the family's experiences. Today, by the marriage of Cunninghame Graham's great-niece Jean to Henry Hepburne-Scott, the Baron Polwarth, the Graham lineage is entwined with Sir Walter Scott's.

It was on his mother's side that young Robert inherited his Spanish blood. His mother's parents were Doña Catalina Paulina Alessandro de Jiménez, a Spanish heiress, and the Scottish seafarer (eventually Admiral) Charles Elphinstone Fleeming, who in South America was a mediator between the liberators Bolívar and Páez, and who, home in Scotland, stood as a Radical M.P. His third daughter, Robert's mother, was born in 1828 and lived on until 1925: and she was as sturdy in temperament as in physique. From her, young Robert inherited a voracious appetite for literary and political matters, a critical curiosity about the world, and a skeptical confidence in judgment.

Robert's father was a cavalry officer in the Scots Greys who also bore the customary responsibilities of the wealthy landowner, being a major in the Renfrewshire Militia, a Deputy Lieutenant of Stirlingshire, and a Justice of the Peace. Like his wife, he was a Radical in political outlook and stood (unsuccessfully) as a candidate for Parliament. His career was to be blighted by misfortune. While stationed in Ireland, in hungry provinces which were turbulent after the repeated failures of the potato crop, he intervened in an angry exchange between a passing Irishman and a fellow officer; the Irishman promptly hit his head with an iron-shod stick, fracturing his skull, and this was the probable cause of the madness that afflicted him increasingly in later years. Eventually, separated from his children after violent outbursts, he was to be confined to a remote house in the care of a doctor and attendants.

Young Robert led a peripatetic existence, for the family was constantly traveling from one base to another, spending part of the year on the estates in Scotland, part in London, part in resorts like Ryde on the Isle of Wight, and part on travels around Europe: the normal life-style of the wealthy British gentry in the mid-nineteenth century. Robert came to love the melancholy wilds of Scotland around Gartmore: the heather-clad hillsides where the deer and grouse flourished, above the chilly gray lochs and icy trout-streams. His formal education was provided by Dr. Bickmore's preparatory school at Leamington and subsequently by Harrow—the private school which had nurtured Lord Byron and which shared with Eton the reputation of being the most exclusive (and expensive) of the monastic boarding-schools for the sons of the rich. Here at Harrow, Robert gave early evidence of the athleticism that kept him fit and agile into old age: he played cricket, won cups for running and jumping, and enjoyed racquets and swimming. With academic work, however, his progress was disappointing, and the Head complained that the young Robert was irreverent in chapel (perhaps the first hint of that atheistic irony which was to glint among many subsequent pages). Another omen was an early essay of his which denounced cruelty to men and to animals as a sign of cowardice and decadence. He responded well to patriotic indoctrination: "I remember being stirred almost to enthusiasm when I was informed that wherever the British flag floated, all were free and equal before the law, irrespective of race, position, or colour" (*IK, 3*).

After Harrow, Robert's education took place in London and Brussels (where he took lessons in Spanish and sword-fencing) and on a walking-tour of Switzerland with his genial private tutor, Mr. Gulliver, whose antiracialist views were later published in a poem. Robert belonged to a family of intrepid travelers: his father had journeyed into the wilds of Croatia; an uncle had won a medal in the Crimea; another had fought tribesmen on the northwestern frontier of India. And Robert's imagination had also been stirred by the adventurers of his childhood reading. "Visions of Drake, of Hawkins, and of Captain Kidd, of Aaron Burr, of Claude du Val, Jack Sheppard, Xenophon, Sir Walter Raleigh, and other noble spirits, who launched their barques into an unknown sea in hopes to find the Indies, rise and excite our minds" (*IK, 6*). The brave and brutal explorers in the pages of Mayne Reid troubled his imagination. And preserved among his papers to this day is a boy's adventure tale, "Rambles of Tom Bainbridge" from *Kingston's Annual for Boys,* which tells how young Tom sailed from Liverpool to New Orleans and defended various underdogs—a poor lad, a black slave—from arrogant Americans. Robert was later to take the same route and a similar moral stance. Tom says: "None but a madman, like the Knight of La Mancha, runs a tilt against windmills when travelling in foreign lands. Still, I say, do not do at Rome as the Romans do, and protest, if not loudly, silently—by your conduct— against vice and immorality, and all the abominations you may meet with."[5]

In May 1870, when he was still only seventeen years old, Robert sailed from Liverpool to the River Plate on the S.S. *Patagonia.* From Montevideo, traveling first on river steamboats, then on horseback through rough country, he reached the Estancia de Santa Anita, owned by an emigrant Scot, James Ogilvy. Robert was supposed to learn the art of ranching; he certainly learned about civil war. He wrote home that there was a revolution in progress, preventing him from traveling up-country. "Ogilvy & another Escoces [Scot] having had all their cattle killed, horses destroyed & lost everything by the war are going about the country buying hides & wool & making immense profits. . . . . They have proposed to take me into partnership. . . . ." (PC; *WD,* 17). The whole region was turbulent with confused civil warfare following the murder in April 1870 of Justo José de Urquiza, constitution-maker of the Argentine Republic and patriarchal governor of Entre Ríos, by raiders led by López Jordán. Hacking at him with knives, the raiders had pursued Urquiza around the vulgar opulence of his ballroom: "as he dodged about the meretricious glass-topped tables the blood dripped on the marble floor," until he fell. (Long afterwards, seated peacefully by a campfire beneath the stars, one of the murderers told Robert the story. See "San José," in the volume *Progress.*)

Robert's time in Argentina, repeatedly subsidized by money from home, combined intrepid tourism with cattle-ranching and horse-droving. One such horse-droving expedition took him some 300 miles from Gualeguaychú to the town of Córdoba, in the direction of the Andes, as he explained to his mother in a letter:

Seeing that horses are very scarce there on account of the great quantity of foreigners that are in the city to see the exhibition & the inroads of the Indians who carry off all they can lay their hands on, I have therefore bought thirty or forty horses at twenty dollars apiece & hope to sell them there at about eighty or a hundred dollars each. . . . . Poor Don Diego who has lost all of his cattle horses & everything else with the war has taken to drinking & is in a state bordering on Delirium Tremens. His brother and I have been trying to get him out of town but it is no use. I have just come from the part of the country called the Ibicuy an old Indian camp. It is quite the most curious country I ever saw. Sometimes you have to go for miles crawling through the thick woods leading your horse[;] the woods are perfectly swarming with humming birds. . . . . I had a very bad fall the other day from a wild horse. . . . . (PC; *WD,* 20)

During these and subsequent travels, the inquisitive young Scot was evidently storing his memory with the sights and sounds that he would recall so vividly in his writings of thirty, forty, or fifty years later: in those pages which today form one of the most sharply detailed memorials of life on the pampas, among the gauchos and settlers of Uruguay, Entre Ríos, and Argentina. He saw how men who rode like centaurs nevertheless waddled like ungainly alligators when on foot; and he never forgot such characters as the *gaucho haragán,* the solitary rider with his lean horse and rusty iron spurs. This character would call at the house for a glass of water and make a cigarette without dismounting, chopping the tobacco from a lump with a knife a foot long, holding the cigarette-paper between his bare toes till the tobacco was fine enough; "cursing his horse if it moved, yet annoyed if it stood still, his glance fixed on nothing apparently, yet conveying to you somehow that it took in everything of value." Did he want work? "No, Señor." Was he going anywhere? "Nowhere in particular." Where would he sleep? "Where the night catches me." Had he no arms except that knife? "No, Señor. God is not a bad man." He would ride off, carrying a piece of meat tied to his saddle, his torn poncho fluttering in the air. Robert adds: "Usually the morning after his visit a good horse had disappeared, or a fat cow would be found dead—killed for his supper." (See "A Vanishing Race" in *FA*, 168–69.)

Once, in a forest between Villeguay and Nogoyá, in Entre Ríos, Robert met two brothers jogging along on horseback. One brother was upright and swaying with his horse; the other "just as upright, tied in his saddle to two sticks"—a corpse riding to the cemetery at Gualeguay. It is typical of Graham's range of experience and leaps of memory that he should have recalled this incident about a quarter of a century later when reading an ancestor's chronicle of 1687 which appeared to refer to a ride by a deceased Scottish Earl (*ND*, 49). Another example of these leaps is that, as an aging man sipping turtle soup, Graham would be reminded of the Indians of Bahía Blanca. "Their choicest delicacy was the fat piece along a young colt's neck; this they ate always raw, and I remember once having to taste it in response to a compliment addressed me by a young warrior, who yelling 'There's a good Christian,' thrust the fat dripping meat into my unwilling hand. The effect was lasting, and to this day I cannot look on a piece of green turtle fat floating in the soup without remembering the Indian delicacy" (*H*, 30).

Subsequently, many legends were to circulate about Robert's adventures during these early years in South and Central America. One legend was that he was captured by revolutionaries and forced to fight on their side; another was that he was seized and bound by Indians, but escaped after killing his guard; and another was that he took a wagon-train of cotton from Texas to Mexico, sold it at a loss, but recouped by establishing a fencing-salon which became a great success with all the fashionable people of Mexico City. All these legends have a degree of plausibility. As we have seen, he did travel in regions disturbed by revolutions and by Indian incursions; he did reach Mexico and was a qualified sword-fencer. The more melodramatic aspects (the double capture, the fashionable salon), however, appear to stem largely from the imagination of A. F. Tschiffely, the early biographer who wished to emphasize the glamour of Robert's career.[6] The truth was less melodramatic but still impressive enough in its range.

There is no reason to doubt that Robert took part in skirmishes against the Indians who devastated the ranchers' estates, and he soon had ample knowledge of violence whether political or domestic, although he quite likely embellished the yarns occasionally as a favor to friends and relatives. Consider this letter home in which he describes "an old campañero" of his:

Bill Rice had been forty years in this country & was the best fighter with the knife in this part of Spanish America. Previously to my going home he gave me a letter to post in England the first he had written for 40 years, which I posted. He got an answer telling him he had had some money left him & determined on going home to Dartmouth. . . . . In the course of bidding his friends goodbye he happened to go to the house of one Repton an Irishman who happened to be drunk & was going to indulge himself in the national luxury of beating his wife[.] Bill interfered . . . . . the Irishman seized his knife & stabbed him to the heart killing him instantly. Such is life in the River Plate.[7]

He recalled later that when riding with a friend from Tapalque to the Sauce Grande, he passed house after house sacked and burned by the Indians, or the occasional estancia surrounded by a ditch and full of women and wounded men. "We camped on the Arroyo de los Huesos, swam the Quequen Salado, buried a man we found dead at Las Tres Horquetas, and after a week's riding, through camps swept clear of cattle and of mares, came to the Sauce Grande just in time to take a hand in a brief skirmish and see the Indians drive off the few remaining horses in the place" (H, 32–33).

In 1873–74, Robert worked in Paraguay as a surveyor and agent in the *mate* trade. (*Mate* is a herb which yields a refreshing bitter drink resembling green tea.) Here he explored some of the most remote and dangerous regions: the Upper Paraná, for example, a wilderness where cougars roamed and travelers ran the risk of being hit by blowpipe-darts from the recesses of the woods. The depopulation of the country had allowed the cougars to multiply so rapidly that Robert and his guide, after feeding their horses, had to sleep alternately, the waker holding both horses hobbled and bridled. As a consequence of the disastrous war fought by Paraguay against Brazil, Argentina, and Uruguay, the population had fallen, it was said, from one and a half million to a quarter of a million: so many of the men had died that much of Paraguay was in a state of gynarchy, with women running the villages and doing much of the work—including engine-driving—formerly done by men. Another anomaly awaiting Robert was that in the most wild and jungle-conquered areas, he frequently encountered the crumbling relics of Spanish civilization—the ruined missions and chapels established centuries before by the Jesuits. He saw richly gilded organs, broken and cobwebbed, which held colonies of bats, while the carved pulpits were inhabited by scorpions and snakes (*PD,* 14).

After the Paraguayan exploration, Robert collaborated as a rancher and horse-trader with his ex-naval friend George Morton Mansel, their most arduous venture being to drive a hundred horses through jungle and across rivers from Uruguay into Brazil, where their hopes of making a fortune were soon dashed—mules rather than horses were in demand there. None of Robert's trading ventures prospered: not ony did he fail to make his fortune, but he consistently spent and overspent his private allowance. The pennies and shillings regularly handed over as rent by Duncan McKeich, Peter McOnie, and the other villagers on the estates in Scotland were being spent on saddle-gear and horses on the other side of the world. George Auldjo Jamieson, Curator of the Graham estate, keeping the accounts in his immaculate hand, from time to time drew the attention of posterity to the fact that the prodigality of Mr. Robert was one of the main reasons for the increasingly perilous state of the finances: a characteristic entry is: "This deficiency arises from sundry extra payments made on account of Mr. Robert C. Graham beyond his allowance of £250. . . . ."[8] Certainly Robert's expenses often exceeded those of both his brothers (Charles and Malise) together, for in the 1870s he traveled to Iceland, Gibraltar, and Nova Scotia as well as to South America.

His brother Charles, born in 1853, had become a naval cadet after leaving Harrow, and subsequently served on the frigate *Ariadne,* the royal yacht *Osborne,* and the flagship *Royal Alfred.* Eventually he became an official of the Royal National Lifeboat Institution and was commended for his zealous rescue work, helping to save the crews of two vessels in a storm. He was appointed groom-in-waiting to King Edward VII and to King George V. His death, from aneurism, came in 1917. In turn, his son Angus entered the Royal Navy and saw active service in both world wars. As Admiral Sir Angus Cunninghame Graham he became the heir to the Cunninghame Graham estate.

Of the three brothers (Robert, Charles, and Malise), the youngest was the unfortunate Malise, who was born in 1860 but suffered poor health and was to die of tuberculosis in 1885. After schooling at Winchester, he entered Oriel College, Oxford, as a theology student. For a while he then served ably as a curate at St. John's

Church, Winchester, before his failing health sent him, without avail, in search of the sun abroad. Robert was often to express antimilitaristic and skeptical opinions, but that did not prevent his enjoying cordial relationships with both his brothers.

Meanwhile, in 1878, Robert made a dramatic change to his own condition. Having returned to Europe from America, he met, eloped with, and married at the Strand Register Office in London, Gabriela (Gabrielle de la Balmondière), a sensitive, introspective, imaginative girl with dark, brooding eyes. This sudden marriage to the nineteen-year-old daughter of a Chilean merchant caused the family considerable surprise and shock, and it is doubtful that Gabriela ever felt that she had really been accepted by Robert's mother ("my dreadful M. in L.," as her diary puts it).

Characteristically the honeymoon was an arduous one: Robert took his nineteen-year-old bride to New Orleans, Brownsville, and Corpus Christi. He bought a hundred acres of land to farm at Nueces Bay, but soon became disgusted by Texan life—particularly by what he termed "the meanness, hypocrisy & assassination" of the citizens. He complained: "I don't believe in Italy in the Middle Ages there was so much assassination as there is in Texas today. Every day there is one or two, such a thing as a fair fight is unknown, & if you enquire how so n'so was killed, 'I guess Sir—waited for him in the Chaparral & shot him in the back Sir' " (PC; *WD*, 43). He also detested the press's response to Indian incursions. "Notices appear in the newspapers in large type. Death. Blood. Scalps. The Indians again. Citizens to the front. Pray to God. Hallelujah. Why is it both in England & America when white troops win it is a victory & when beaten is it termed a horrible massacre. I always thought a massacre meant when the massacred could not resist."[9]

The couple stayed for a while in San Antonio and eventually traveled on by wagon-train to Mexico City: a dangerous journey on which Robert, believing that there was a plot by the captain to rob and kill him, carried a revolver, a twelve-shot Winchester carbine, a knife, and a sword. Other impediments to the joys of the honeymoon were provided by Indians. Gabriela subsequently recalled that on arrival at Juárez, the couple had found that Mescalero Apaches had murdered a local family and burned their hut. The mother and ten children had been killed; one survivor was a little boy who had crawled into the bushes. "We talked over the dismal occurrence at night over the camp-fire, the coyotes howling dismally in the distance, as we sat round smoking cigarettes and endeavouring to chew hunks of tough dried meat, before wrapping ourselves in blankets and going to sleep. . . . . Before turning in every rifle was put ready to hand, and the animals carefully staked." At the roadside Gabriela saw a bloated corpse hanging from a tree.[10]

During this period Robert attempted further ranching ventures, but with the customary lack of success; he was more a tourist than a settler, although the tours covered much interesting territory— he even, on one journey, met and made friends with Buffalo Bill at Horsehead Crossing,[11] a friendship that was renewed many years later when Bill's Wild West Show reached London. Nevertheless, the estate's curator found that in America, Robert and his wife had incurred debts of nearly £2,000. (At this time, a laborer with a wife and seven children could survive on £50 per year.)

On the death of his father in 1883, Robert inherited the family home and the estates of Gartmore, Ardoch, and Gallangad. Like a scene from a George Eliot novel of provincial society was the "Complimentary Dinner" given to the new laird by the tenantry and feuars on the estates. The Rev. Irvine of Gartmore spoke; so did the Chairman, the Lord Provost of Glasgow; and other notables were Sir Donald Currie, shipping magnate, and Mr. Orr-Ewing, M.P. Various tenants rose to welcome the new landlord and to express the hope that he would not become an absentee, while Robert, with mild irony, suggested that "this auspicious meeting" might be "the beginning of a new order of things."[12] On the wall behind him were displayed the arms of the Grahams (neatly worked in holly leaves) with their motto, "For Right and Reason." But when the euphoria of that public welcome was over, there remained the wearisome responsibilities and worries of the landowner. After deductions for interest on mortgages, family annuities, taxes, up-keep, etc., the income was substantial. As time went by, however, and agricultural prices fell, while the expenses of the laird and his wife (both addicted to traveling, whether together or separately) remained heavy, Robert found it increasingly difficult to maintain the estates, particularly as his political commitments grew. Inter-mittently both he and Gabriela worked hard on the management of the lands, pruning the costs, arranging drainage, haggling with dour cottagers; but the struggle proved futile. First, Ardoch was auctioned (later, part was bought back). Then the great house of Gartmore, its rooms smelling of kingwood furniture and damp, became increasingly leaky and dilapidated, and eventually the historic house and its lands had to be sold; a bitter fact for a man so keenly nostalgic and aware of the traditions of the past.

Politics. But Robert Bontine Cunninghame Graham was a man of paradoxes. If in many ways he strove to keep the past alive, in others he was an innovator, an iconoclast, a pioneer of social revolution. On becoming domiciled in Scotland he, like his father and grandfather, had taken to radical politics. After a zealous campaign in the heavily industrial constituency of North-West Lanark, he was elected to Parliament in July 1886; and although he was nominally a Liberal, he soon revealed himself to be the first Socialist in the House of Commons. His maiden speech startled the House by its stylishly sarcastic denunciation of the monarchy, of British imperialism, and of capitalism. One reporter noted: "House kept in continuous roar for more than half-an-hour. Fogeys and fossils eye him askance, and whisper that he ought to be 'put down'; but lovers of originality, in all quarters, hail him with satisfaction."[13]

Graham, an elegant patrician speaking in the soulful, world-weary tones of a sophisticated aesthete, brought into British parliamentary life an eruption of radical and left-wing ideas. During his six years in Parliament (1886–1892) he condemned imperialism and racial prejudice, corporal and capital punishment, profiteering landlords and industrialists, child labor, religious instruction for schoolchildren, and the House of Lords; and he advocated the eight-hour working day "in all trades and occupations," free education, Home Rule for Ireland and Scotland, and the nationalization of every industry. Although he could be a stylishly ironic and even Puckish speaker, he was also capable of losing his temper spectacularly if he thought that parliamentary procedures were being used to stifle his pleas for suffering humanity. On three occasions he was ordered by the Speaker to withdraw, and his defiant retort "I never withdraw!" is re-echoed by Saranoff in Shaw's *Arms and the Man*.[14]

There has been a tendency of commentators (Garnett, Conrad, Tschiffely, Bloomfield, and MacDiarmid among them) to suggest that Graham was a *frondeur,* a spirited humanitarian but not a Socialist. For a crucial period of his life, their assessment is wrong. During those parliamentary years he was an avowed Socialist, and arguably, because of the publicity that his prominence gave to the cause, the most important Socialist pioneer in England at that time. When asked in Parliament whether he preached "pure unmitigated

Socialism," he replied, with promptitude and coolness, "Undoubtedly."[15] Histories of the Labour movement generally give the impression that the first Socialist in Parliament was Keir Hardie (a man of the working class—so he fits left-wing mythology better), but if we judge by contents and not by labels, that honor is definitely Graham's. Hardie did not enter Parliament until Graham had left it, in 1892; and, in any case, Graham was Hardie's political mentor and was crucial in steering the cautious ex-miner toward Socialism. Hardie (a fellow Scot) was particularly impressed by Graham's advice that a working-class representative in Parliament should wear his ordinary workday clothes and use plain working man's language; "above all, he should remember that all the Conservatives and the greater portion of the Liberals are joined together in the interests of Capital against Labour."[16]

According to Emrys Hughes, Graham's first meeting with Hardie took place when Graham rode into Cumnock (probably in 1887) on a magnificent black horse which he halted outside the humble tenement where the Hardies lived in a room and a kitchen. They talked about miners' conditions and the Eight Hours campaign, and Hardie offered to take Graham down a nearby mine. Graham agreed. "The two men crept on hands and feet through a long subterranean passage to the coal face where a man, stripped to the waist, his body covered with sweat and coal dust, was working alone. When the two men came out into the fresh air Hardie said, 'Cunninghame Graham, there's no muckle [i.e., not much] in our civilisation after a'.' "[17] When Hardie and his miner friends sat in the Public Gallery to watch parliamentary debates, Graham would join them to explain the procedure and identify the main figures, referring to the House as "The Thieves' Kitchen" and "The National Gas Works," and observing that "the strife of parties means nothing but a rotation of rascals in office"—the only difference between Conservatives and Liberals being "the better cut of the Conservatives' boots." Hardie corresponded with Gabriela, praising her writings ("so full of heart and so exquisitely dreamy") and her campaigning: "It is not often one sees such a Combination of Heart and Intellect," he said of her speech on behalf of poor crofters.[18] Cunninghame Graham, who in Parliament championed miners and their pit ponies, sponsored Hardie at election time and supplied material for Union newspapers edited by the ex-miner.

Graham had entered a Parliament dominated by two big parties: the Conservatives, who now held power, and the Liberals, who were divided against themselves over Irish Home Rule; there was a small group of Irish patriots, led by Charles Parnell; and there were some "Lib-Labs"—working men who voted with the Liberals. What was needed—so Graham argued with increasing force on platforms and in left-wing journals—was a parliamentary party dedicated specifically to meeting the needs and aspirations of the working class: a Labour Party. And with this end in mind, in 1888 he helped to launch the Scottish Labour Party, the first such in Britain. He was elected its president, while Hardie became secretary. Their program included nationalization of transport, minerals, and banking, a graduated income tax, national health insurance, free education, and the abolition of the House of Lords. Cunninghame Graham, as an M.P., was the new party's most influential spokesman.

It can be argued, of course, that Graham was then acting unethically, because he had been elected as a Liberal and should therefore have resigned and sought reelection under the Labour banner he had raised (in which case he would almost certainly have been defeated). It has also been suggested that by professing views "that were little short of revolutionary" while still being nominally a Liberal, Graham "helped to sustain working-class faith in Liberalism"[19] and may thus have retarded the cause of Labour. The journals of the time had no difficulty, however, in identifying Graham's real allegiances. The *People's Press* called him "the only member of parliament who can really be called a Socialist," explaining that there he looks "just as we have seen him on a hundred platforms pleading the cause of the Docker, the Gas-worker, the Railway Man, the Shop Assistant, or any other worker that needs his help, with that native eloquence and evident sincerity that has won the hearts of the 'unskilled labourers' " (26 April 1890, 3).

Critics who think that Graham was a poseur, a flitting amateur of politics, are refuted by the record of his tireless campaigning over the years. In that parliamentary period he campaigned up and down the country on behalf of the exploited chainmakers of Cradley Heath (among them, women, children, and old men, struggling in squalid workshops for a bare subsistence); with John Burns and Prince Kropotkin he helped the dockers in their struggle for "The Dockers' Tanner"; and he spoke alongside Friedrich Engels (coauthor of *The Communist Manifesto*), Sergei Stepniak (Russian assassin), and George

Bernard Shaw (Fabian Socialist) at demonstrations for the eight-hour working day. He traveled to Paris with Hardie and William Morris to become a lively multi-lingual participant in the Marxist Congress of the Second International; he was expelled from France after a speech of sympathy with the strikers of Fourmies who had been fired on by the authorities; and he found time to write regular polemical articles for left-wing periodicals like the *People's Press* and the *Labour Elector*. "Who's wrong? What's wrong?" he asked. "Is it employer or employed? Or both? My answer is, the system; the base, vile, commercial system that sees God in gold" (*PP*, 16 August 1890, 9).

Considering that "the system" was one which permitted R. B. Cunninghame Graham to travel the world at will, to dress with aristocratic elegance (top hat, bow tie, cloak, and silver-topped stick), and to pay more for a horse than a working man earned in a year, we might wonder what had led him to give so much of his time and energy to denunciation of it. This was a time of massive unemployment and poverty, of hunger and squalor for many but vast fortunes for a few; and it was a time when urban discontents were being given potent voice by H. M. Hyndman's Social-Democratic Federation, a well-organized revolutionary group which emerged in the early 1880s, from which in turn emerged, after schism, William Morris's Socialist League. (Both Hyndman and Morris were very wealthy men who could subsidize their groups and publications.) Graham worked with both leaders, learning assiduously from them, cooperating more often with Hyndman but reserving more of his affection for Morris—he found appealing the fact that the ebullient Morris not only made furniture but also (in his fits of rage) bit it.

Cunninghame Graham's socialism had many sources: in addition to the militant propaganda of Hyndman and the idealistic anti-industrial visions of Morris, he came to know Edward Carpenter's very influential *Civilisation: Its Cause and Cure;* and he knew the writings of Karl Marx, referring briefly to them in Parliament. As we have noted, he campaigned with Marx's surviving collaborator, the rich mill-owner Friedrich Engels, and has left an affectionate pen-portrait of him during an eight-hour-day meeting in 1890:

Talk of 70 years of age! why he seems more to be seventeen . . . . . , his spirits more buoyant than a youth's. He gives the credit to "K-Ka-

Karl, to my friend Marx"—the voice just trembling for a moment as he thinks of him. Still, he has seen the Chartists, remembers the great stagnation period, rejoices at the great 4th of May meeting of this year, gently chides me for my over-caution, and argues that in ten years' time, if he lives (and there seems no adequate reason why at this rate he should not live for ever), that crowns, principalities, priests, and powers will lie howling, and that the proletarians will rule the roast and eat it. (*PP,* 6 December 1890, 7)

Engels, in return, was confident that Graham was "an enlightened Marxist" and the first Communist in the British Parliament. Graham's pragmatism, however, voiced itself in the comment: "I am a believer in the theories of Karl Marx to a great extent, but, both as regards Christianity and Socialism, I care more for works than faith."[20] A more important influence than Marx was probably the Victorian Radical tradition at its most richly eloquent—in the works of Carlyle and Dickens, with their passionate and memorable indictments of the squalor, injustice, and hypocrisy within bustling Victorian England. Cunninghame Graham's father and grandfather had made ventures into radical politics; he had inherited a sense of *noblesse oblige* and chivalry (and the landowner's traditional jealous hostility to the men of commerce); and above all he had his own urge to champion the underdog, that urge whose tutelary deity was his lifelong literary hero, the incorrigible arch-intercessor, Don Quixote. And, like the knight of La Mancha, Graham found that to tilt at windmills or giants could soon earn a man a bloody head.

He found this out in the affair that gained him his greatest notoriety—the Battle of Trafalgar Square, on Bloody Sunday, 13 November 1887: the battle that Morris mythologized in *News from Nowhere.* On 8 November, Sir Charles Warren, the Chief Commissioner of Police, had prohibited all meetings in Trafalgar Square, hoping by this means to prevent a repetition of the riots by the unemployed which had already resulted in mass arrests; and the decision also had the effect of banning a rally planned by the Metropolitan Radical Federation to demand the release of William O'Brien and other imprisoned Irish patriots. On the afternoon of the thirteenth, thousands of demonstrators, some carrying banners of Morris's Socialist League and Hyndman's Social-Democratic Federation, converged on the Square, which had been cordoned by 1,600 constables. The Square was crowded and turbulent; scuffling and fighting took place there and on the approach-roads. Graham, who had previously declared his intention of defying the ban by making a speech in the Square, had met Hyndman with John Burns and other associates of the S.D.F. leader at Charing Cross Station, and they made their way through the crowds toward the cordons. According to the police, Graham and Burns emerged arm in arm and headed briskly toward their lines, followed by about two hundred supporters; Graham threw his hat into the air and rushed forward with a shout, swinging his fists and punching Police Constable Blunden hard in the teeth.[21] In the subsequent melee Graham was hit on the head and body by truncheon and fists; blood poured from his head, and both he and Burns were arrested and charged with "riot and an assault on the police." Meanwhile the crowds were dispersed by cavalry and by the Grenadier Guards with fixed bayonets.

Among those who fled from the scene was George Bernard Shaw, the militant Fabian. "We *skedaddled*," he told Morris, "and never drew rein until we were safe on Hampstead Heath or thereabouts. Tarleton found me paralysed with terror. . . . . On the whole I think it was the most abjectly disgraceful defeat ever suffered by a band of heroes outnumbering their foes a thousand to one. . . . ."[22]

Bloody Sunday and the subsequent court cases received massive publicity: leading articles in *The Times* denounced Graham for leading "an insane rush" at the head of "howling roughs" animated by "simple love of disorder, hope of plunder, and the revolt of dull brutality against the rule of law."[23] In court, stentorian Burns defended himself with his customary pugnacity; Graham was defended by Herbert Asquith, subsequently to be Liberal Prime Minister. Graham's claim that he had not assaulted the police but had gone like an eager lamb to the slaughter was supported by Edward Carpenter, the homosexual libertarian, and upheld by the jury. Both the defendants were found guilty of "unlawful assembly," however, and sentenced to six weeks' imprisonment, without hard labor, at Pentonville Prison. (Burns was later to be a distinguished cabinet minister in the Liberal governments between 1905 and 1914.)

Graham's notoriety was now complete. To many workers and political militants, he would long be remembered as the hero of Bloody Sunday, the champion who had physically assailed the oppressive establishment; to some other people, he would be remembered as a wild man, a law-breaking eccentric and publicity-seeker, a traitor to his class.

After the grim weeks of prison, where he was constantly hungry and where, ironically, his main consolation was the communal hymn-singing in the chapel, Graham returned to Gartmore pale and thin; the people of the estate unharnessed the horses and themselves drew his carriage home amid cheering and applause. Prison did not diminish his militancy; on the contrary, he continued to campaign throughout the country, and remained a controversial and sometimes angry parliamentarian, while his wife, Gabriela, spoke at meetings to further socialism and feminine emancipation—this in the 1880s and 1890s, before the Suffragettes were on the scene.

In 1892 his term in Parliament ended: he stood unsuccessfully as a candidate for the party he had done so much to create: the Labour Party. But although he failed to be reelected, he continued his political battles on platforms and in essays, letters, and articles published in a remarkably wide range of periodicals, including Hardie's *Labour Leader,* Hyndman's *Justice,* and Frank Harris's *Saturday Review.* He attacked economic exploitation at home, and imperialism (whether by Britain or the United States) abroad. After 1900, as the Labour Party grew in numbers in Parliament, he became increasingly critical of Labour M.P.s, feeling that they too often became tame and respectable: "I tell them . . . . . that they would do more good if they came to the House in a body drunk and tumbling about on the floor."[24] He continued to support Labour candidates at elections, however, and in his oratory he emphasized that he sought a social revolution—even a violent one, if necessary. He was excited when, in 1911, social and industrial unrest reached such a pitch that Home Secretary Winston Churchill responded to a wave of strikes by putting the nation under military control, with troops marching into London and all the main provincial centers. At Liverpool, where the docks and transport were paralyzed, thousands of strikers battled with the police, and two were killed by the soldiers' bullets. "Sheer anarchy," cried *The Times;* but Graham applauded the workers, saying that they now had the chance to "hurl the Government from power."[25]

The social unrest of those years in Britain was ended partly by the government's negotiations and largely by the outbreak of the First World War. On 2 August 1914, Graham, Hardie, Hyndman, and Ben Tillett headed a huge demonstration in Trafalgar Square to denounce Britain's impending entry into the war; yet within a few weeks, Graham tried to enlist in the army, in spite of being far too old for recruitment (he was sixty-two). His patriotism had been aroused by the German violation of Belgian neutrality and by reports of atrocities there. Eventually the War Office sent him to South America as head of a team to select and buy horses for the troops fighting in Europe. He worked harder than ever before, often on horseback from dawn to dusk, soaked with rain and dew, lassoing and sorting the animals in corrals knee-deep in mud. ("However I find it more artistic than any literature, & am still quite up to it," he told his friend Rothenstein.[26]) All his life, Graham had opposed cruelty to animals. He fastidiously eschewed fox-hunting and disliked bull-fighting; he had drawn Parliament's attention to the plight of pit-ponies; and he had even expressed his compassion for the pangs of netted fish. So it was a bitter irony that he should now be selecting the horses which were to suffer, and in many cases die, amid the gas and shrapnel of the Western Front. He knew it; and he recorded his regrets in the essays "Los Pingos" and "Bopicuá."

Later Years. The melancholy, elegiac tone of such essays had sounded with increasing frequency in his writings since 1900; and there were obvious reasons for this. In 1900 he had been obliged to sell Gartmore, his decaying ancestral home. (It was bought for £126,000 by Sir Charles Cayser, the shipping magnate. Today it is a reformatory for delinquents, managed by Roman Catholic priests. Where once Robert and Gabriela sat reading beneath portraits of the august ancestors, teen-agers now play snooker beneath posters of popular singers.) Six years after the sale of Gartmore came a worse blow, when Gabriela died in France at the age of forty-five. She had long been consumptive, suffering wretchedly but bravely from lung ailments exacerbated by her addiction to cigarettes; the frequent journeys to the hot sun of Spain and Italy sometimes helped and sometimes exhausted her. She was brought home by Robert for burial on the island of Inchmahome, in the ruined church of the priory. The inscription that he chose for the plaque beside her grave was: *Los muertos abren los ojos a los que viven* ("The dead open the eyes of the living"); and perhaps her writings (romantic poems, translations, essays, and an eloquent two-volume biography of Santa Teresa) still, occasionally, open on her and on the past the eyes of those who live now. Robert and Gabriela had held much in common, including a love of nature, the picturesque past, and the warm south; but they had often journeyed separately, and their marriage was childless.

Another loss came in 1917, when Charles, the seafaring brother, died of a heart ailment; now both Robert's younger brothers were gone. Former fellow campaigners were going, too. In 1915 Robert stood beside Tom Mann and Bruce Glasier at the cremation of Keir Hardie, and mused: "Had he, too, lived in vain, he whose scant ashes were no doubt by this time all collected in an urn, and did they really represent all that remained of him?" (*BF*, 58).

Yet, after the 1914–18 war, Cunninghame Graham returned to what he termed the "dunghill" of politics. In spite of all his previous attacks on the Liberal Party as the party of commercial ruthlessness and pietistic hypocrisy, he stood as a Liberal candidate in 1918, opposing a Labour man as well as a coalition candidate at West Stirling. He conducted a lively and entertaining campaign, advocating Home Rule and "the nationalisation of the mines, shipping, and eventually of all means of production,"[27] and denouncing Bolshevism, conscientious objectors, and the House of Lords. National trends favored the coalition candidate, and Graham came bottom of the poll to him: the end of his last stand as a parliamentary candidate.

In the remaining years of his life, Graham devoted his political energies increasingly to the cause of Scottish Home Rule. He had come to feel some disillusionment with the Trade Union movement and with the Labour Party, which he now regarded as "a party struggling for office and place like any of the other parties": whether they were Labour men, Tories, or Liberals, they were "the same dogs with different collars," he felt. He became president of the National Party of Scotland, and of its successor, the Scottish National Party, whose supporters included several well-known writers—Hugh MacDiarmid, Compton Mackenzie, and Eric Linklater.

In two ways, he was thus returning to his roots. He had journeyed to far-off places; but now, in his patriotic speeches at Stirling, where the party held its annual rallies, he could dwell on his ancient Scottish ancestry. He could also take pride in the fact that half a century previously he had been the first Member of Parliament to put the case for Scottish autonomy before the House. So there was, after all, a consistency of endeavor in his career. His romantic side now found ample expression, as when, in 1930, he addressed the crowds from his platform at Stirling, the winds ruffling his white hair:

The eternal hills still form our background. Stirling Castle, a perennial monument to the power of Scotland when she shook the might of England to the core, makes our middle distance. Not far from where we are to unfold this banner is the historic Borestone whence the banner of the Bruce fluttered on the greatest occasion whereon victory has crowned the arms of Scotland. Three miles from here Wallace broke Cressingham upon the long bridge over the Forth. Where'er I look, north, south, east or west, there is something that appeals to me as a Scotsman, there is something to stir one's heart, something to make one feel that we are representatives of a distinct nationality—a nationality severed from all other nationalities and as different from our friends in England as we are from the Germans, the French, the Russians. . . . .[28]

If at times he was romantic (and even sentimental and illogical), he was also a humane realist who, in old age as in youth, was appalled by the filth and squalid poverty of the slums of Glasgow and by the endemic unemployment of Clydeside; he knew that Scotland had too long been the poor relative of England. On the Continent, Nationalist politics flourished in the 1920s and 1930s, and had brutal and genocidal consequences; but Scottish nationalism was a small and innocuous force, and it is reassuring that Graham, late in life, referred contemptuously to Mussolini's bombing of Abyssinia and enthusiastically to the downfall of Primo de Rivera in Spain. Graham was leader of the Scottish Nationalists until his death in 1936. Since then, the Scottish National Party has been more often dormant than dynamic; but in a phase of popularity in the mid-1970s it certainly showed that, like other of Graham's underdogs, it had stamina and a capacity for growth and bite.

Further Travels. In the foregoing pages we have concentrated on his political career, but Graham's "first career" as a traveler should not be forgotten. After those early adventurous days in Central and South America he had continued to travel frequently and widely—Iceland, Spain, France, Morocco, Argentina again, Colombia, Jamaica; and these travels contributed in obvious and important ways to both his political and literary careers. His sense of the color, vitality, and apparent freedom of exotic pastoral and nomadic lands made him the more keenly aware of the drab gloom, grime, and wretchedness in the northern industrial nations. Then the travels provided a thousand locations, characters, and ironies to be preserved in his subsequent pages.

An incident which admirably illustrates the ways in which fact and fiction, reality and fantasy, life and art, travel and literature could all intertwine is the gold-prospecting interlude of 1894. One day at Gartmore, when Robert and Gabriela were browsing through an old Spanish edition of Pliny the Elder's *Historia Naturalis* (written in the first century A.D.), Gabriela was excited to find that a passage describing an old Roman gold-mine in Lusitania seemed to refer to a locality in Spain that she knew well. She traveled out, and, accompanied by an experienced prospector, T. J. Barnard, made her way to the remote, wolf-haunted hillside near Carraceido. She took ore from the site to a chemist at Villafranca for the preliminary assay: some grains of gold actually appeared. Now it was Robert's turn to come out and busy himself, bumping into Carraceido in an ancient mule-drawn diligence, arriving at a bug-infested inn, and making a donkey-ride by moonlight to the site. Below him, a great bowl, a quarter of a mile across, seemed to have been dug from the red earth; chestnut trees grew in it, and here and there towered up great pinnacles of earth capped by bushes, "making them look like some fantastic vegetable." "The moonbeams played upon them, magnifying and distorting them, and striking here and there upon a pebble in their sides, which sparkled brilliantly. So still was everything that we stood looking, awestruck, till the guide, advancing cautiously up to the hedge, held out a lean, brown finger and said, 'That is the Roman mine' " (*H,* 170).

Eventually a mule was loaded up with two big sacks of earth and they were taken to the Mining College of Madrid for the full assay. Graham's hopes faded to nothing as firing proceeded to its drossy end. Yet although the sacks yielded only dust, the fires of imagination could smelt from the experience some literary gold—Graham's tale "A Page of Pliny" (in which he is thinly disguised as "McFarlane") and Conrad's novel *Nostromo,* that epic about the consequences of the reopening of an ancient Spanish silver-mine by Charles Gould, a character based (as Norman Sherry[29] has shown) on Cunninghame Graham.

Graham's Influence

Another example of the ways in which life and literature interwove so that Graham's material failures became literary successes in his or other writers' pages was, as we shall see later, the Tarudant expedition, when Graham's abortive attempt to reach this "Forbidden City" in Morocco yielded his own best travel book, *Mogreb-el-Acksa,* and prompted Shaw to write *Captain Brassbound's Conversion.* Not only did Graham's travels inspire other writers; his very character and appearance, which were an incentive to etchers, painters, and sculptors (Strang, Lavery, Rothenstein, Toft, and Epstein, among others), can be discerned in various literary figures. George Bernard Shaw says that Cunninghame Graham was the model for the dashing, impetuous Sergius Saranoff in *Arms and the Man,* and he may also have contributed some of the more reckless qualities to Hector Hushabye *(Heartbreak House)* and Dick Dudgeon *(The Devil's Disciple).* In Joseph Conrad's works, Graham's features can be seen not only in Charles Gould in *Nostromo* (another red-haired, proudly equestrian treasure-seeker and traveler in the Americas) but also in Mr. X, the elegantly aristocratic firebrand of the tale "The Informer" (in *A Set of Six*). If we turn to *The Inheritors* (1901), a novel written jointly by Conrad and Ford Madox Hueffer, we find that the narrator and central figure is a man of distinguished and ancient family, an author ahead of his times, who, by permitting the publication of an antiimperialist article, abets the disruption of the British political establishment. Although he is by temperament (passive and drifting) a marked contrast to Cunninghame Graham, a link is suggested by his aristocratic lineage, his subversive role, and the sound of his name—Etchingham Granger, which clearly echoes that of the Scottish writer. Certainly a noted critic has suggested that Etchingham Granger "is of course Cunninghame-Graham" [sic].[30] In John Galsworthy's novel *The Patrician* (1911) appears the wiry, red-haired Mr. Courtier, the quixotic "knight-errant" and "champion of lost causes"; and given that Galsworthy corresponded with Graham and published admiring reminiscences of him in *Forsytes, Pendyces and Others,* a debt to the Scot seems probable.

As we have seen, Graham also corresponded with H. G. Wells, who was interested by him but regarded some of his writing as rather wild (he had described the preface to *The Canon* as "indiscreet and bickering"); so it may not be entirely coincidental that the hero of Wells's *When the Sleeper Wakes* (1899) is called Graham and is described as follows: "He was a man of considerable gifts, but spasmodic, emotional . . . . . he took up politics of the rabid sort. He was a fanatical Radical—a Socialist—or typical Liberal,

as they used to call themselves, of the advanced school. Energetic—
flighty—undisciplined. Over-work upon a controversy did this for
him. I remember the pamphlet he wrote—a curious production.
Wild whirling stuff. There were one or two prophecies. Some of
them are already exploded, some of them are established facts."[31]

A different kind of debt was acknowledged by John Masefield,
the author of tales, essays, novels, and poems, who became Poet
Laureate in 1930 and is today best remembered in England for
"Reynard the Fox." Between 1907 and 1910, Masefield had an
enthusiastic, flattering correspondence with Graham: the young
author claimed that "The Captive" (in *Hope*) was "quite the best
modern story I know." Sending him a copy of *A Tarpaulin Muster*,
Masefield said: "In these tales I have imitated everybody, just as,
in my other books, I have done my best to imitate yourself."[32] This
is further evidence that although Cunninghame Graham's books
never reached a wide public, he was certainly a "writer's writer"—
one whose works (as well as whose ways) were closely studied by
fellow craftsmen.

Another linkage is indicated in a letter from Edward Garnett to
Graham dated 23 November 1898. "My dear amigo, that you should
have brought Conrad & Nordau together is a stroke of genius.
Nordau! and Conrad!"[33] Joseph Conrad—the most intense, dedicated, anguished novelist of the times, admirer of Flaubert and
Maupassant, just entering his major phase; and Max Nordau, author
of the best-selling controversial work *Degeneration*, which denounced
the decadence of contemporary culture and suggested that *Uncle
Tom's Cabin* was a better work than *Madame Bovary*. Nordau had
read and admired Conrad's *Nigger of the "Narcissus"*, and he had
asked his acquaintance, Graham, to forward his letter of praise to
the author. Max Nordau was a disciple of the Italian criminal an-
thropologist Cesare Lombroso; and it is notable that subsequently
Conrad's *The Secret Agent* was to make extensive ironic use of Lombroso's theories of atavism, degeneration, and conspicuous criminal
typology; perhaps the contact with Nordau had prompted this
development.

Certainly, as Garnett's reference to the "stroke of genius" reminds
us, one special "career" of Cunninghame Graham was that of cultural
go-between, linking and aiding the most heterogeneous groups of
people. There were painters like Lavery and Strang, Whistler, Rothenstein, and Augustus John; political individualists, adventurers,

and mavericks—the Irish patriot Parnell, Lawrence of Arabia, the humanitarian Roger Casement (who died a traitor's death), the antiimperialistic diarist Wilfrid Scawen Blunt; naturalists like W. H. Hudson and Henry Salt; pioneer Socialists and militant trade-union leaders—Ben Tillett, Will Thorne, Keir Hardie, Tom Mann, John Burns, and later Jim Larkin; revolutionaries like Hyndman, Engels, and Morris; courtesans and prostitutes like "Elise" or the *chinas* and *peyne d'oro* girls of Argentina, who are often recalled in his pages; the assassin Stepniak and the anarchist Kropotkin; cowboys and gauchos like Buffalo Bill, Miguel Paralelo, and Pablo Páncharo; novelists—Wells, Conrad, Ford, Galsworthy, Henry James; critics—Garnett, Arthur Symons, Edmund Gosse; explorers—Up de Graff and C. H. Prodgers; poets—Hardy, Masefield, Ezra Pound; cartoonists—"Spy," Max Beerbohm, Harry Furniss; prime ministers—Asquith and Ramsay MacDonald; sculptors—Toft, Jacob Epstein; editors—Frank Harris *(Saturday Review),* W. T. Stead *(Pall Mall Gazette),* A. R. Orage *(New Age),* Ford again *(English Review);* playwrights—Wilde, Shaw, Henry Arthur Jones; the actor-impresario Martin Harvey; scholars, historians, convicts, naval men, circus hands. No wonder that Conrad exclaimed: "What don't you know! From the outside of a sail to the inside of a prison!"[34] Graham was a questing cosmopolitan of the cultural world as well as of the geographical.

Literary Career

Although he led a remarkably full life as a political pioneer, as a traveler, and as a social celebrity, he still found time for a literary career which was of considerable plenitude and richness. Many factors helped to turn his thoughts to writing. His ancestor "Doughty Deeds" was an anthologized poet—admittedly on the strength of one well-known poem of gallantry. His father, William, wrote poems that were often wistfully romantic in quality; and his mother was an alert, vigilant reader with strong and independent critical opinions—scorning the mystical and pietistic, she thought Wordsworth overrated, for example. From his early years, with her encouragement, Robert had been a voracious, rapid, pouncing, and retentive reader with a taste for the vivid, original, and offbeat as well as for many of the traditional masterworks; he avoided the merely fashionable and detested the commercial.

He liked works with a tang of salty realism or irony, including the *Canterbury Tales* of Chaucer, writings by Donne and Traherne, the *Verdadera historia* of Bernal Díaz, Cervantes's *Don Quixote* (of course!), Shakespeare's *Hamlet*, de Rojas's *Le Celestina*, stories by Mark Twain, Maupassant's tales, and, later, Turgenev's shorter works, particularly *A Sportsman's Sketches*. His political writings were to be peppered with allusions to Shakespeare, Dickens, Carlyle, Dante's *Divine Comedy*, and the poetry of Alexander Pope and Ben Jonson. In 1872 he was consoled by Spenser's *Faerie Queene* during a storm-tossed voyage from Europe to the River Plate; with the gauchos of Bahía Blanca he took turns to recite *Martín Fierro*, the folk-epic by José Hernández; and in 1875–76, he and his friend Mansel found Fitzgerald's *Rubáiyát of Omar Khayyám* "a great consolation" during another transatlantic crossing. In later years he would enjoy Stevenson's "Christmas at Sea" and Wilde's "Ballad of Reading Gaol." Writing home from Corpus Christi, Texas, in 1879, Robert comments mockingly on the quality of new religious rubrics and quotes Swinburne's notoriously pagan "Hymn to Proserpine"; and, while in San Antonio, he was reading Villon's poetry, Palgrave's *Golden Treasury* of verse, and biographies of Hume, Voltaire, and Las Casas. George Moore's recollections (in *Conversations in Ebury Street*) of the Graham who liked to discuss with him the life and work of Verlaine and Rimbaud seem entirely plausible.[35] Graham's range was extended by his fluency in Spanish and French and by his knowledge of some German, Italian, and Portuguese: when he quoted Villon and Dante it was in the original tongue. If frequency of allusion is an indication, one of the most important influences on this skeptical Scot was the Bible; and three of his eventual sketches ("The Impenitent Thief," "The Fourth Magus," and "The Dream of the Magi") were to be extended meditations on biblical events.

Although it is customary to remark that Graham's writings stemmed largely from those early years of travel, it is at least arguable that the travels stemmed largely from his early reading (whether about Mungo Park or Tom Bainbridge) and had in part a literary motivation—a desire to store a mind with experiences which would furnish tales. A crucial model for emulation was the work of the prolific American writer Bret Harte (1836–1902). As early as 1876, Graham wrote home to his mother from South America: "Decidedly it is reserved for me to be the Bret Harte of the South, but in

Spanish or English?" In another letter, the Bill Rice anecdote (quoted previously) is introduced thus: "I will tell you the story of the death of an old campañero of mine which for wildness equals anything of Bret Harte's." While in Texas in 1879, he wrote from Corpus Christi: "I think there is a street here that would lay over anything in 'Red Dog,' the place is very like one of Bret Harte's places, the same loafers pingos Mexicans etc., & the same intermixture of Germans & French."[36] And by 3 July 1880 he was reporting that he had tried, unsuccessfully, to make a magazine article out of his Mexican journey.

With "The Luck of Roaring Camp" (1868) and other tales of California and the frontier, Harte had "shaken gold from the grass-roots." Harte's work had become popular and influential: his yarns of the gamblers, prospectors, drunks, whores, and storekeepers, told with descriptive fluency and (in the dialogue) vernacular gusto and boldness, captured the democratic imagination by their combination of humor, realism, and sentimental pathos. These tales (rather like his harlots, who had thick skins but soft hearts) ostensibly displayed harsh, vulgar life but insidiously imparted the cheering doctrine that the coolest gambler and roughest miner would happily lay down their lives for a babe or lost maiden.

Graham evidently admired the picturesque range of "characters" to be found in Harte's pages; he would certainly have sympathized with Harte's skepticism about religion, with his humanitarian concern for society's waifs and strays, and with his indignation against racial prejudice. "The sincere volunteer soldiery of the California frontier were impressed with the belief that extermination was the manifest destiny of the Indian race": the quotation is from Harte's "The Princess Bob and Her Friends," but even in its tone and phrasing it could equally well have come from one of Graham's subsequent pieces. In 1890 Graham actually sent long letters to the London *Daily Graphic* denouncing the genocidal treatment of the North American Indians by the authorities, and offering the warning that the Indians might in desperation make a last massive uprising. He asked the American writer to join him in the protest, and Bret Harte replied:

I hope you will believe that I cordially enter into your feelings in regard to our Indian troubles, even though I cant [*sic*] see my way, just now, to their expression. It is the old story of our Anglo Saxon Civilized aggression,

yet I have thought that during the last fifteen years of our Indian Admin-
istration, it has not had to be told so often, and I have been hoping that
it was of the Past. Of course the disire [*sic*] to "improve" people off the
face of the Earth with a gun, and then to punish them for learning how
to use the weapon will continue to exist, yet I think that my Western
friends have lately forborne to act up to their doctrine that "the only good
Indian was a dead one."[37]

Thus, from various quarters—family tradition, his own literary
appetites, and the crucial example of Bret Harte, chronicler of frontier life—Graham was impelled toward a literary career. His preference for the shorter, more anecdotal literary forms was confirmed
by his admiration for the South American tales of W. H. Hudson
(particularly "Niño Diablo," which he read in 1890) and for the
Argentinian vignettes of Alfred Ebelot's *La Pampa*. This preference
happily matched the need of many magazine editors for "middles"—
for stories, essays, reminiscences and descriptive pieces—particularly if, in this heyday of European imperialism, they dealt with
remote and exotic regions. Graham's first tales appeared relatively
late, when he was over forty, in the 1890s, but the flow of material
grew steadily, and by the time of his death in 1936 he was the
author of sixteen volumes of tales and essays. Furthermore he wrote
a guidebook, two travel books, eight biographies, three histories
which (like most of the biographies) related to the Spanish Conquest
of America, and various translations, including a rendering of
Rusiñol's Catalán play *La Verge del Mar*. Then there were eight
pamphlets or booklets, at least fifty prefaces to works by other
authors, hundreds of uncollected items in newspapers and magazines, and reminiscences to be included in other people's books; not
to mention the posthumous collections of his writings which numerous editors gathered.

As with the life, so with the works: the first impression is of a
rather bewildering variety, with contrasts and even contradictions.
Ferociously sardonic political polemics; self-consciously literary pen-
sive meditations; accounts of lesser-known conquistadores; character-
studies of relatives or bizarre passing acquaintances; a defense of the
Jesuits in Paraguay; tales of brothels and prostitutes; elegiac obituary
studies; lore about horses or the flora and fauna of Spain, Morocco,
and South America; reflections on the Moslem empire of the past;
tales of exotic passion and violence; and tones ranging from the
satiric to the scholarly, from the melancholy to the whimsical.

As with the life, so again with the works: the second impression is of a complex unity: and the secret of the unity is, of course, Graham's sympathy with the underdog—Graham's determination to fight for justice in an unjust universe. Thus he sides in his writings with the underdogs of imperialism—downtrodden races or individuals of those races; with the underdogs of capitalism, the hard-pressed workers; and with the underdogs of society—the prostitutes who were hypocritically reviled by a society which found them indispensable. In his biographies and histories, he had a taste for neglected areas and figures. He sympathized with the eccentrics and failures, the flotsam and jetsam of the tide of "progress," and with all those distinctive characters of the past who were once vivid but were now forgotten.

Indeed, there were moods in which Graham could regard virtually all humanity as the downtrodden of the universe, since all were sentenced to death without hope of reprieve. As he said to Garnett in 1899: "My view of life is almost the same as yours. It is a joke, a black joke of course, but we must laugh at our own efforts. Escape, too clever. Not I, it is far cleverer than any one, & the wheel will go right over my chest (completely over), as over yours & all." And in *Mirages* (1936) he wrote: "But then, although they tell us that death is the wages of the sinner, as far as I can see, it seems to be not very different for the saint."[38]

Vain, egoistic, and erratic, yet proud, courageous, and gallant, Cunninghame Graham strove to ride like a knight-errant against prejudices of race, nation, and class, against complacency and callousness, against the forces of neglect, oblivion, and death. He always knew that the causes most worthy of defense were not those most likely to succeed, but the extent of his successes, in life and literature, is somewhat greater than subsequent generations have recognized. His political campaigns found gradual fruition in later years, as the Labour Party came to govern Britain, as the trade unions grew in power, as the eight-hour day became the norm, as the rights of women gained recognition, and as the British relinquished their empire and gave independence to the colonial lands; and his uneven writings, too, living in the imaginations of responsive readers, may yet keep his vigorous personality alive as a force for good in the world. His monument at Dumbarton called him "A King among Men—A Master of Life"; and a survey of his works will help us to recognize the truths within these fine hyperboles.

Chapter Two
Earliest Writings

Cunninghame Graham's writings up to 1900 are characteristically diverse. He began, of course, with political polemics: reports, reviews, and controversial articles in journals and magazines; then followed, naturally enough, political pamphlets. But soon he produced a work of a very different kind: his first book, *Notes on the District of Menteith,* 1895. Between 1896 and 1900 appeared several volumes of tales; and in 1898 appeared the travel book which some writers have deemed his masterpiece: *Mogreb-el-Acksa.*

Political Journalism

Graham was a prolific contributor to political debate in the press, whether as a reporter of meetings, as a controversialist, or as a reviewer of other men's writings. Between the late 1880s and 1900, well over a hundred such items appeared in print. The periodicals which published him ranged from extreme Socialist publications like William Morris's *The Commonweal* and Hyndman's *Justice* to the Liberal *Pall Mall Gazette* and the staid *Speaker;* others were the *Labour Elector* (of which Graham was one of the owners), the *Labour Leader,* the *People's Press, Contemporary Review, Star, Labour Prophet,* the *Albemarle, Time* (London), *Living Age* (Boston), the *Nineteenth Century,* the *Saturday Review,* the *Pageant,* the *Daily Chronicle, Westminster Gazette,* the *Social-Democrat, Freeman's Journal* (Dublin), *Journal of the Knights of Labor* (Philadelphia), and the *Glasgow Herald.*

A vast output, and most of it utterly lost, save to those scholarly time-travelers who in libraries search the flaking pages of the past. Yet in those pages, gradually, history was being made; the "climate of opinion" was being modified in a thousand infinitesimal ways by this article and that. And for some of those time-travelers, Graham's pieces provide refreshment in the deserts of print. His polemical work generally was—and often remains—sharp, lively, and distinctive. The sharpness is a matter of intelligence, for he could think and write incisively; and it is also a matter of his political radicalism, for he presented extreme left-wing views with an almost insolent confidence and ease, at a time when such views were still utterly heterodox to the vast majority of the British public.

He repeatedly argued the need for an eight-hour working day (eleven or twelve hours being quite customary then), for militant trade unionism (particularly on behalf of unskilled workers), and for the foundation of a Labour Party. His concern for the underdog made it quite consistent that he who reported (and took part in) the great dock-strike at Liverpool in 1890 should in the same year be writing to the *Daily Graphic* on behalf of the North American Indians. Similarly, while advocating the eight-hour day in the columns of the *Labour Elector,* he was also informing its readers, in a series of "Foreign Notes," about life in Spain, Portugal, Brazil, Argentina, Cuba, Mexico, Florida, and Italy.

Part of the pleasure for present-day readers may lie in the encounter with ideas which (as Edward Garnett noted) seemed more than fifty years ahead of their time. Even those people who may not share his views or appreciate their contemporaneous value for that past era may still see that he could be an attractive polemicist, able to write rapidly and spontaneously, yet with a certain stylish self-consciousness. This passage from his "Open Letter to Prince Krapotkine" well conveys the flavor, as Graham defends socialism from the attacks by Anarchists:

I want to know, my dear Prince (of Anarchy), why it is that so many Anarchists (not yourself) assume so pestilent a tone of superiority over the rest of the world? You know I hate labels, and care not a fig whether a man calls himself an Anarchist, Socialist, or Liberal, or even Tory, so that he be going my way. I am equally indifferent as to his religion. If a man bows before his Joss, turns his praying-wheel, or even if his religion be confined to taking whisky in his tea (like the Irishman's grandmother) it is all one to me.

Still, though[,] it is undoubted that you (I mean the Anarchists) have not charity. Passion o'me! how you do pound us in the *Révolte* and the rest of your press! Has it never occurred to you that we are not a bit more in love with Government neither of the people nor by the people than you are? We look on Government as a hideous necessity, and intend to endure it as short a time as possible. We look for a time when Government shall become so perfect that we can do without it. I mean that we hope by means of Socialism to make men fit for Anarchy. (*Labour Elector,* 15 February 1890, 109)

There is the direct, vigorous address; there is the element of epigram (as in that last sentence); a tinge of quirky ironic humor ("whisky in his tea"); and a salting of literary archaism, an echo of Hotspur or Pistol ("I . . . . . care not a fig"; "Passion o'me!"). And in the peroration that follows, two further characteristics: a lapse in syntax (perhaps the result of hasty composition or his barely legible scrawl) and an unexpected, leaping simile: "If, therefore, we can prepare the poor and miserable to realise that a state in which, whilst each owning nothing, yet all will be rich, shall not we have deserved well of you? We are labouring for the same cause as you, and have undertaken the rough and dull, day by day labours of convincing and preparing so that your Pegasus, when he descends to earth, shall find provender ready for him, and not like the horse Cortes left with the Indians on his expedition to Guatemala, die of hunger amid wreaths of flowers."

Graham produced a number of pamphlets whose usual destiny was to be sold for a penny per copy at Socialist meetings and demonstrations: *The Nail and Chainmakers* (probably 1889), *Economic Evolution* (1891), and *The Imperial Kailyard* (1896). The first of these (which had three contributors) includes Graham's plea for the chain-makers of Cradley Heath near Birmingham, people who toiled in the grimmest conditions of "domestic industry," hammering hot iron into nails and chains, for what in some cases was not even a bare subsistence. Here Graham writes with an eloquence that may owe something to William Morris or Marx, but probably more to Carlyle and Dickens:

> Let me try to place before you Cradley Heath.
> A long, straggling, poverty-stricken, red brick, Worcestershire village. Houses all aslant, with the subsidences of the coal workings underneath. Houses! yes, houses, because people live in them. But such dens! Ill-ventilated, squalid, insanitary, crowded; an air of listlessness hanging on everything. Not a pig, not a chicken, not a dog to be seen. A fit place in which to preach thrift, and economy, and abstinence! Oh, yes, especially abstinence—but from what? . . . . .
> The crowded little workshop, with its four or five "hearths", its bellows, its anvils, its trough of black water, its miserable baby cradled in a starch box. The pile of chains in the corner, the fire of small coals, the thin,

sweating girl, or boy, or old man (every one seems either very young or very old at Cradley, age seems to follow so hard on youth). The roof without ceiling, the smell of bad drainage, the fumes of reeking human beings pent in a close space—such is a Cradley Heath workshop.

Mud, dirt, desolation, unpaved streets, filthy courts, narrow reeking alleys, thin unkempt women, listless men with open shirts showing their hairy chests. Mud, dirt; dirt and more mud—such is Cradley Heath as regards its streets.

Work, work, always; ever increasing; badly paid; from early dawn till after dark; from childhood to old age, and this is the chain they forge. . . . .

To sum up the position briefly. Failure of civilisation to humanise; failure of commercialism to procure a subsistence; failure of religion to console; failure of Parliament to intervene; failure of individual effort to help; failure of our whole social system. [1]

Like Dickens, Graham can utter the rhetoric of rhythmic iteration and can show misery and squalor graphically, with an eye for telling detail (here, the baby "cradled in a starch box," for instance) and ironic symbolism ("this is the chain they forge"); but unlike Dickens, Graham at the end of the denunciation will proceed to suggest specific legislative measures for improving the lot of the workers at Cradley Heath: either municipal control or establishment of a Co-operative Society there. Graham had revolutionary moods and anarchistic ideals, but he was also prepared to give time and work to immediate reformist programs. As he had told Kropotkin: "Would you, if you were a workman, prefer your stalled Anarchist ox and eleven hours a day, or your dinner of herbs and Eight-Hours legislation? I trow that at the end of the Eight you would enjoy your papiros [*papirosa*, Russian for "cigarette"] with more satisfaction." [2]

The second pamphlet, *Economic Evolution*, had its first edition in 1891 and was later republished (as *An Irish Industrial Revival*) by the Irish Socialist Party; it also appeared as an article, "The Evolution of a Village," in *Albemarle Magazine* in 1892 and in the collection *Success* in 1902. It is one of the simplest pieces of Socialist propaganda that Graham wrote: the story of an imaginary Irish village where the people, although poor, live in contentment, until their lives are transformed by the coming of capital and the establishment of a factory. "Capital had come. . . . . It banished peace, idleness, beauty, and content—made slaves of the people." [3] This rather banal fable has an agrarian nostalgia which recalls the outlook of Graham's fellow campaigner William Morris. Criticizing the propagandistic naiveté of the piece, H. F. West remarks drily: "[O]ne knows that girls in villages have 'accidents' before eighteen, and that they are not all due to the 'closeness of boys and girls in hot rooms' " (*HFW*, 94–95).

More interesting is *The Imperial Kailyard,* a scornful attack on imperialism in general and British imperialism in particular. It claims that although we are conditioned from youth to admire conquerors, "In stern reality the 'native' is the hero, and the European 'conquistador,' as Beit, Barney Barnato, Selous, Rhodes and Co., nothing but cowardly interlopers, presuming on superior weapons." Our missionaries have the obligation to instruct the natives "that the first duty that a Matabele owes to Queen Victoria is to stand upright like a man and let our gunners have a chance to play their Maxims [machine-guns] in a proper way upon him," so that at last the British flag will wave over Africa as it does "over the workhouse pauper and the sailors' poor whore in the east end of London."[6]

The same theme is developed in the polemical article which became perhaps the most celebrated of all Cunninghame Graham's shorter works: the essay " 'Bloody Niggers' " (*Social-Democrat* 1 [April 1897]:104–9), which was reprinted as "Niggers" in *The Ipané* in 1899, *Thirty Tales and Sketches* (Edward Garnett's selection) in 1929, and *Rodeo* (Tschiffely's selection) in 1936. This is the piece that led Conrad to say: "You are the perfection of scorn—not vulgar scorn mind, not scorn that would fit any utterance[.] No! Scorn that is clear in the thought and lurks in the phrase. The philosophy of unutterable scorn." And Garnett said of Graham: "The immortal 'Niggers' . . . . . and its fellow sketch 'Success' stamp him, in W. H. Hudson's words, as 'Singularísimo Escritor Inglés,' the most singular of English writers, and they would confer immortality on him if he had written nothing more."[5]

In " 'Bloody Niggers' " Graham attacks centrally the imperialists' frequently-made claim to be carrying out the will of God by taking religion and civilization to far-off lands. What gave the piece its high reputation was the obliqueness of method and the lofty ironic tone. Graham was often to be tempted (sometimes with good results, sometimes bad) by the lengthy, circuitous preamble; and here the opening is characteristically leisurely and devious. He writes as chronicler of the Lord's achievements, as historian of the Creation:

"He (Jahve) created all things, especially the world in which we live, and which is really the centre of the universe, in the same way as England is the centre of the planet, and as the Stock Exchange is the real centre of all England. . . . ." Then follows a grand catalog of the treasures and flora and fauna of the world, the jewels, trees, grasses, animals, mountains and tribes, until the culmination is reached: "God made the earth and made it round, planted his trees, his men and beasts upon it, and let it simmer slowly till his Englishman stood forth"; naturally, the rest of mankind have been created so that the Englishman may prove his mastery over them all. And finally the ironic mask of the urbane historian grows transparent as Graham's humane scorn emerges: " 'Niggers' who have no cannons, and cannot construct a reasonable torpedo, have no rights. . . . . Their land is ours, their cattle, fields, their houses, their poor utensils, arms, all that they have; their women, too, are ours to use as concubines, to beat, exchange, to barter for gunpowder or gin, or any of the circulating media that we employ with 'niggers'; ours to infect with syphilis, leave with child, outrage, torment, and make by consort with the vilest of our vile, more vile than beasts."[6]

Today, as we look back over this piece, we may well find the descriptive catalogs prolix and the ironic stance inconsistently maintained. When we reflect, however, that this essay first appeared in 1897, the year of Queen Victoria's Diamond Jubilee, a year of wild patriotic and imperialistic enthusiasm in Britain, at a time when the nation's most popular literary spokesman was Rudyard Kipling and when the European powers were engaged in the scramble to seize Africa, we may perhaps forgive Graham's vehemence and understand his friends' appreciation.

Early Books

Notes on the District of Menteith. Perhaps it was as a relief from political polemics that Cunninghame Graham wrote his first book, *Notes on the District of Menteith, for Tourists and Others,* which appeared in August 1895. This is his eccentric guide to the Menteith area, where he had grown up (for the estate of Gartmore is part of it); and what makes it eccentric is Graham's egotism. He offers his views of the locality and its characters; and the part of its history that most concerns him is, inevitably, the more picturesque growths of the family tree of his ancestors, the Earls of Menteith, with their claim to be the true Kings of Scotland.

"It is with considerable pain," he says, "that I have to refer to anything that might in any way seem to be an aspersion on the morality of one of our Scottish kings"—the one in question being Robert II of the house of Stuart. "Had it not been for the bad example set by him, Scotland might still have been a moral nation." With relish the author reviews the Grahams' claim to have "blood redder than the king's"; and the book is peppered with his characteristic quirky remarks, variously arch, facetious, cynical and ironic, on history and human nature. Though the district may seem remote and tranquil, "a kind of sea of moss and heath, a bristly country . . . . . shut in by hills on every side," it is threatened by the leveler, "progress," which destroys the more interesting features of the past (whether thatched cottages or the Gaelic language) and replaces them with a dull uniformity. "Gaelic is gone, or only just remembered by the elder generation, yet it gave the names to all the burns and glens and lochs; names curious and descriptive, like the names the Indians give to places in America. It may be, when all are numbered, Ben Number One, Loch Number Two, and so on, that even Gaelic will become a thing to be regretted." Even the rugged men of the region are gone: "The hunters and the hawkers, the livers by their spurs, ... are buried and forgotten, and the tourist cracks his biscuit and his jest over their tombs."[7]

The tourist who is lured by the subtitle to buy the book as a topographical guide may be sometimes more bemused than enlightened by it, given its numerous speculations and reflections of a whimsical and occasionally facile kind. Nevertheless, this modest volume was quite generously reviewed (by *The Times, Guardian* and *Athenaeum,* for example) as an amusing, entertaining, and lively book. *The Times* (6 September 1895, 10) said:

Mr. R. B. Cunninghame Graham's *Notes on the District of Menteith* . . . . . is avowed by its author, in a preface addressed "to the disingenous reader," not to have been "penned for the general benefit of mankind, nor, as far as I know, to increase knowledge, either scientific or theological." Perhaps, indeed, he wrote it mainly to please himself and air his reflections on things sundry and various in the guise of a series of chapters on the district of Menteith and its associations, personal and historical. These reflections on men and manners, places and events, are often rather wayward and whimsical, but not seldom shrewd and pithy withal, and "tourists and others" who are properly attuned to Mr. Cunninghame

Graham's peculiar and rather exotic vein of humour will find not a little
to attract and entertain them in his "unambitious," but far from commonplace, "booklet."

The admirer of this work, then, may bear some resemblance to the
old Scottish lady cited by Graham, who, having claimed that apples
grown in Scotland were the finest in the world, added, "I maun
premise I like my apples sour."

  Father Archangel of Scotland. In the following year appeared
Cunninghame Graham's first collection of short pieces: *Father Archangel of Scotland, and Other Essays* (most of them by himself, some
by Gabriela). The reader soon discovers why his short items were
commonly called "sketches": it is because that term, one fashionable
in his day, is sufficiently vague to embrace their generic range: tale,
reminiscence, travel essay, etc.; and it also arouses appropriately
modest expectations (of work which may be deft but slight, rapid
and unpolished). In this volume, the locations are characteristically
exotic—Spain, Paraguay, Argentina, Morocco—and the emphasis
is characteristically autobiographical. Even when he is summarizing
the life of some bygone character (Father Archangel himself, for
example), Graham is strongly to the fore, commenting in humorous
or melancholy tone on that career. The collection is given some
unity by the recurrent theme of transience.

  As we have noted, Graham throughout his life was profoundly
troubled by the idea that just as an individual may be lost without
trace in a jungle, so men of the past, leading worthy lives, may be
lost to history by the force of oblivion, and so people of the present
may be ignored and forgotten for want of a due memorialist. As
politican, Graham fought for the underdog; and as writer, he defends
numerous underdogs in the endless fight against time, change,
decay, and forgetfulness. Thus Graham's socialism was linked, par-
adoxically, to a profound conservatism. He himself, at an imaginative level, made the connection: for when Belfort Bax, the Socialist
editor of *Time* magazine, asked him for an article advocating the
eight-hour day, Graham submitted instead "The Horses of the Pampas," an essay celebrating the gauchos and horses of South America:
the link being that Graham saw them as dying breeds which were
gradually being extirpated by that very industrial civilization whose
rigors needed to be mitigated by eight-hour legislation. He wrote
(*FA,* 164–65):

The races at the Pulperia, the fights with the long-bladed knives for honour and a quart of wine, the long-drawn melancholy songs of the Payadores, the Gaucho improvisatores, ending in a prolonged Ay—celebrating the deeds and prowess of some hero of the Independence wars—these things, these ways will disappear. Gaucho and horse, Indian with feathered lance, will go, and hideous civilisation will replace them both. In their place will rise the frightful wooden house, the drinking-house, the chapel, the manufactory. Those who are pleased with ugliness will be contented. Those who, like myself, see all too much of it already, may regret that light and colour, freedom and picturesqueness, are so rapidly being extirpated from every corner of the world.

At least we may be allowed to express the hope that in the heaven the Gaucho goes to, his horse may not be separated from him.

In *Father Archangel*, related pieces are "A Vanishing Race," describing the various types of gaucho encountered by Graham in his early days; "In the Tarumensian Woods," which describes the relics of the old Jesuit colonies in Paraguay (an interest begun during Graham's explorations in 1873–74 and which culminated in his *A Vanished Arcadia*); and "El Babor," which tells how the traditional way of life in an Arab town is being changed for the worse by the introduction of a modern mill powered by steam (the *babor,* or "vapor," of the title). Given this theme, there is often an elegiac tone to the writing; and one of the tales, "Ras Doura," is indeed a melancholy account of a traditional Moorish funeral.

Another recurrent preoccupation of these (and subsequent) pieces is with religious faith—particularly with the embattled faith of missionaries who, like Father Archangel in Calvinist Scotland or the Jesuits in Paraguay, seem destined to fail. Again, it is a seeming paradox that the skeptical Graham should, throughout his career, have been so fascinated by men of militant faith; and the explanation lies not simply in his familiarity with the contrast between the dour Protestantism of the Scots and the Catholicism of the warm, Spanish-speaking lands. Graham was an affectionate connoisseur of the absurdities of human nature; and to him, both a skeptic and an idealist, there was something ludicrous yet heroic about men who strive arduously and give their lives for beliefs which defy reason. And there was a darker explanation of Graham's enduring preoccupation with such men. As an idealist and a skeptic, he could feel that centrally there was no difference between those Catholic missionaries and *any* person who strives for a moral ideal. If, as Graham felt, there were no absolute, metaphysical, or historical guarantees of the success of any moral principle, then any moral idealist was a person working by faith in the dark jungle of human experience. Long before the term "existentialism" was known, Graham was exploring his intuition of moral conduct as a human assertion against the nonhuman void.

These themes that we have noted—the dying race, the poignant labor of faith, the lonely individual engulfed by a wilderness—all combine memorably in what is probably the best tale in this first collection, "A Jesuit." Like most of Graham's works, it is based on personal recollection: in this case, of a journey by steamboat up the rivers Paraná and Paraguay in 1872, on which the boat was joined by a modest, solitary figure "dressed in rusty black" whose sole luggage was a newspaper filled with cigarettes. This person is a Jesuit priest, sole survivor of a Paraguayan mission which had been attacked by Indians; having made his way down to Buenos Aires, he had telegraphed to Rome for orders, "and one word had come: 'Return.' " So now, at a clearing in the forest, the steamboat stops and the Jesuit goes ashore at his old haunt. "Stepping ashore, he stood for an instant, a little figure in rusty black, a midget against the giant trees, a speck against the giant vegetation. The steamer puffed and snorted, swung into the stream, the Jesuit waved his hand, took up his newspaper of cigarettes and, as the passengers and crew stood staring at him from the decks and rigging, walked into the forest" (114).

This early collection is uneven; some of the pieces are very slight and amateurish; and the success of "A Jesuit" is a modest one. Nevertheless, it shows that Graham had already found the techniques which were to sustain so many of his later tales. These were, first, the use of a leisurely descriptive opening, an elaborate scene-setting, followed by a homing-in on some figure in the foreground or on some stark visual image; and second, the combination of romantic exotic location with realistic mundane detail, as here: "The river, an enormous yellow flood, flowing between high banks of rich alluvial soil ever slipping with a dull splash into the stream. . . . . The air was full of the filmy white filaments like cobwebs which the north wind always brings with it in those countries, and which clung from every rope and piece of rigging, making the steamer look as if she had run through a cotton manufactory. . . . . Gauchos . . . . . played at 'Truco' with cards as greasy as bits of hide, and so well marked on the back that the anxiety of the dealer to conceal their faces seemed a work of supererogation" (104, 105, 106). It is Graham's readiness not to glamorize but to note the greasy cards, the mosquitoes, the bolts that will not slide, that lends authority to the recollection. At a time when so many magazines and bookshelves carried travelers' tales of exotic regions, Graham's recollections were more sharply focused than most and carried a notably stronger charge of philosophical implication.

It is not surprising, then, to learn that the novelist Graham Greene was, in his earlier years, an admiring reader of Cunninghame Graham's work.[8] Some common preoccupations of the two writers are with "the success of failure" (the idea that an apparently wretched, failed person may have inner dignity or even sanctity) and with the juxtaposition, often in exotic locations, of the noble and the base, the sensitive and the sordid. Both writers value those who, by living dangerously, call into question a prudentially bourgeois ethic. The nicotine priest of Graham's "A Jesuit" may be a forebear of the whiskey priest of Greene's *The Power and the Glory*.

Aurora la Cujiñi. This booklet (1898) marked an advance or foray in the direction of fiction. Although it is based on a personal recollection by Graham, who is present as narrator, the piece flirts with the supernatural. It tells how on a May evening in Seville, after the excitements of the bullfight, the crowds at a low dance-hall are aroused by the dancing of Aurora la Cujiñi—a flamenco dancer of the 1840s who has evidently returned from the past to put present-day dancers to shame by her erotic intensity. Although there is this supernatural element, the piece still earns the adjective in its subtitle, *A Realistic Sketch in Seville,* for in the initial panoramic survey of the city, Graham gives particular attention to the cruel carnage of bullfighting ("The horses . . . . . had trodden their entrails") and its perversely aphrodisiac effects: "from the plaza a scent of blood and sweat acting like a rank aphrodisiac upon the crowd, and making the women squeeze each other's sweating hands, and look ambiguously at one another, as [if] they were men; and causing the youths, with swaying hips and with their hair cut low upon their foreheads, to smile with open lips and eyes that met your glance, as [if] they had been half women. Blood, harlotry, sun, gay colours, flowers and waving palm trees. . . . ."[9]

The account of Aurora herself emphasizes sexual arousal: at the climax of her frenzied dance, "she stands a moment quiet, as it is called 'dormida,' that is, asleep, looking a very statue of impudicity. The audience remained a moment spellbound, with open mouths like Satyrs, and in the box where sat the foreign ladies, one has turned pale and rests her head upon the other's shoulder, who holds her round the waist. Then with a mighty shout the applause breaks forth. . . . ." (We may recall that Graham's wife, Gabriela, who was a guest in Spain of the feminist writer Emilia Pardo Bazán, was sufficiently excited by such dancers to hire one troupe to perform for herself alone.)

Initially, editors found *Aurora* rather too hot to handle, and when it eventually appeared (as a booklet in a limited edition) the publisher was Leonard Smithers, whose *Savoy Magazine* had provided a platform for the Aesthetes and Decadents of the period, including Aubrey Beardsley, Ernest Dowson, and Arthur Symons, the propagandist of the Aesthetic and Symbolist movements. Symons himself wrote to Graham from Seville to praise the tale ("You have the quality which few people have of making one read *with excitement*") and to offer a rival portrait of a Spanish dancer in a poem he had just composed. Edward Garnett, too, applauded Graham's defiance of Victorian Puritanism:

Only an "impression" you will say. Yes, but something that transfers the intoxication *to us*: you infect us with the snaky poison of that woman, the delicious madness. Admirably seen, admirably felt, admirably described! amigo: for the strange emotion works in us too, & that is why the great lords of literaryism, the Henleys & Whatnots (so Conrad told me) looked askance on your cunning pages: it was because *Aurora* is so successful that these Overlords looked round saying "Lord a mussy where *am* I?" This *must* "be pernicious because I really *feel!*"

Oh what idiocy! Roughly speaking the Anglo-Saxon nature condemns all feeling not conducive to its dry salter's code of preserved virtue!

And as for Conrad—his praise was unstinting: "C'est, tout simplement, magnifique. . . . . This seems the most finished piece of work you've ever done."[10]

Today, the piece may seem relatively tame: predictable rather than shocking. That is because, since 1898, so many taboos have faded, so many barriers of censorship have crumbled; and as Graham was one of the countless people who helped to inaugurate the present era of cultural liberalism, we should, in fairness, help *Aurora* by recalling that it appeared in the times of joyless Sabbaths, of Wilde's disgrace, and of repressive pieties.

The Ipané. At that period, Edward Garnett, then working for Fisher Unwin, was the most brilliantly perceptive of publishers' readers. Garnett's acumen has become legendary: it was he who helped into print Joseph Conrad, Galsworthy, D. H. Lawrence, Hudson, W. H. Davies, and numerous others; and he had the gift of creative provocation—he coaxed, prodded, and challenged his writers to give of their best, and they, appreciating Garnett's intelligence and sensitivity, rose to the challenge. For years, he had been reading with pleasure Graham's contributions as they appeared in the *Saturday Review.* As an atheistic radical, Garnett liked Graham's skepticism and his anti-imperialistic bias, which offered so strong a contrast to Kipling's treatment of equally exotic regions. Partly in the hope of offering a counterblast to Kipling, Garnett persuaded his employer, Fisher Unwin, to launch a series called "The Over-Seas Library," which would offer tales of the outposts; then, with flattering letters, he invited Graham to select and revise pieces to be gathered for the first volume in the series. That was how their friendship began. Graham was moved by Garnett's request, replying: "I am glad you like my stuff, for I am, & have been a man of action all my life (& like Cervantes, at some distance off, 'mas versado en desdichas que en versos' ['better versed in adversities than in verses']), & writing came to me with grey hair."[11] Then followed an enthusiastic, detailed correspondence about the material, with Garnett urging Graham to pare his work, to make it coolly ironic and economical, and praising him for his vivid details, particularly the incongruous or revealing image. With tact and sound judgment, he tried to nudge Graham away from the casual and prolix and toward a more deliberate and controlled kind of writing.

In a letter of 23 January 1898, for example, he praises a coordinating image in the tale "S.S. *Atlas*": "The bird-cages, those bird-cages show the hand of the cunning artist. It is the touch which makes the picture live, always live: those cages are a centre, a symbol amid the welter & jumble of the steamer life you so well describe. And to your style such a centre of meaning however tiny, is very necessary, for you are so near life itself in your best writing, that one is in danger of being at the mercy of the action, (steamer, convict cell, Paraguayan plain or what not.) I love those bird-cages!

Do you catch my meaning?" And, on 30 June 1898, he said of "Fraudesia Magna" (a *Saturday Review* article on Rhodesia which eventually was not selected for republication): "I think, your account would be more likely to *live*, if it had a little more wrist-play & a little less of battering blows: if its tone were quieter, more ironical, even congratulatory! it would be more dangerous."[12]

The collection which was assembled under Garnett's aegis was *The Ipané*, 1899. (The title is the name of a paddle-steamer in the first tale and of a Paraguayan town.) The pieces have a characteristic range in setting and in genre: locations include Argentina, Texas, the West African coast, Paraguay, Tangier, Scotland, and Iceland. The elegiac, obituary element is strong: "With the North-West Wind," for example, commemorates William Morris, who had died in 1896, while even the essays "The Lazo" and "The Bolas" have an elegiac undertone in the concluding suggestion that Graham is recalling a South American culture that "progress" is rendering extinct. This attack, on a progress that means urbanization, racial prejudice, and the imposition of European uniformities on exotic cultures, is maintained in various ways throughout the volume, most polemically in "Niggers" (a revised version of " 'Bloody Niggers' "), more subtly in "At Torfaieh" and "Tanger la Blanca." The sketches soon remind us that Cunninghame Graham's political criticisms of European ways combine the aesthetic with the primitivistic. The aesthetic, as usual, lies in his horror of the drab ugliness of the cold industrial north when compared with the bright lands of the sun: better feudal Morocco with its goat-herds than urbanized Europe with its factories. The primitivist's sense that the healthy life must be an unsophisticated one (perhaps ignorance is bliss) and that if there be a golden age its location is far more likely to be in the past than in the future is one that Graham shares with various other writers of his age: with Samuel Butler, Walter Pater, Conrad to some degree, and D. H. Lawrence. In an empirical era when reflective thought provides depressing vistas, the appeal of the instinctual or antirational grows proportionately.

If Garnett hoped that Graham's anti-imperialistic outlook would make *The Ipané* a counterblast to Kipling, he would have been more than gratified by the tale "Bristol Fashion" (the title is a seaman's idiom meaning "Neatly Completed"), in which Graham's opposition to Kipling is both explicit and implicit. The implicit opposition is evident in the exposure of civilized hypocrisy in this story of

"Honest Tom Bilson," skipper of a ship that trades on the West African coast. At home in England, he is a respectable, married chapel-goer; but on his ship he swigs gin while his black concubine bellydances for him. When some of his native crewmen steal a boat, he recaptures them and takes vengeance (which he deems to be sanctioned by the Bible) by selling them to cannibals. " '[B]y Gawd's help I ketched 'em and sold 'em to a chief of one of them cannibal set-outs of niggers down Congo way; fixed 'em, I did, you bet, in Bristol fashion' " (142). Graham's opposition to Kipling becomes explicit in the opening survey (written before Conrad's *Heart of Darkness*) of white men's lives on the coast. "Flies and mosquitoes made life miserable, men took the fever overnight, were dead by morning, buried at gunfire, and none seemed happy but the 'snuff and butter' coloured children, who swarmed in evidence of the philoprogenitiveness of the members of what Mr. Kipling calls 'the breed.' No nonsense about Bilson, 'shipshape and Bristol fash,' and 'treat a bloody nigger well if he works well; and if he kicks, why then speak English to him,' was the burden of his speech. Philanthropists, with missionaries and those who talked of equal rights for all mankind, he held as fools. . . . ." (132).

"Bristol Fashion" is not one of Cunninghame Graham's best tales (Bilson is too gross a caricature, as the quotations may suggest), and although the comparison with Kipling emphasizes the greater humanity of Graham's outlook, it does also draw attention to Kipling's greater technical proficiency and imaginative confidence as a literary artist. Nevertheless some readers—Shaw to the fore—were happy to cast their votes for Graham. Shaw said in 1900: "His tales of adventure have the true Cervantes touch of the man who has been there—so refreshingly different from the scenes imagined by bloody-minded clerks [Kipling had been a clerk in India] who escape from their servitude into literature to tell us how men and cities are conceived in the counting house and the volunteer corps."[13]

If opposition to Kipling gave animus to Graham's tales of outposts, opposition to the Kailyarders gave animus to his accounts of Scotland. "Kailyard" means "Scottish cabbage-patch," and in the 1890s the term "The Kailyard School" was applied to a group of writers who gained great popularity by their anecdotes of Scottish rural and provincial life. The group included J. M. Barrie, "Ian Maclaren" (The Reverend John Watson), and the Reverend Samuel R. Crockett: they liked to record with patronizing affection and some sentimentality the petty feuds and domestic tragedies of the Scottish villagers. Here, for example, is the ending of Maclaren's tale "In Marget's Garden." The dying student, George, prays for his old teacher, Domsie:

> There was a thrush singing in the birches and a sound of bees in the air, when George prayed in a low, soft voice, with a little break in it.
>
> "Lord Jesus, remember my dear maister, for he's been a kind freend to me and mony a puir laddie in Drumtochty. Bind up his sair heart and give him licht at eventide, and may the maister and his scholars meet some mornin' where the schule never skails [i.e., where the school never disperses], in the kingdom o' oor Father."
>
> Twice Domsie said Amen, and it seemed as the voice of another man, and then he kissed George upon the forehead. . . . .
>
> When he passed out at the garden gate, the westering sun was shining golden, and the face of Domsie was like unto that of a little child.[14]

(Even the religiose phrasing—"was like unto"—helps to invite a sentimental stock response.)

Such unctuously tear-seeking pieces explain the bitterness of Graham's complaints in his tale "A Survival": "Then came the Kailyarders, and said . . . . . that they alone could draw the Scottish type. England believed them, and their large sale and cheap editions clinched it, and to-day a Scotchman stands confessed a sentimental fool, a canting cheat, a grave, sententious man, dressed in a 'stan o' black,' oppressed with the tremendous difficulties of the jargon he is bound to speak. . . . ." (*Ipané*, 161–62). And as a realistic counterblast to the Kailyarders, this tale describes Graham's visit to a farm which a new Scottish tenant from the Hebrides has reduced to a squalid rural slum, the man himself being lazy, drunken, incomprehensible, and obsequious, while his ragged daughters sit nearby searching each other's heads for lice. "The fences were all broken, ground untilled, and little zigzag paths traversed the fields where short cuts had been made. The gates were off their hinges, lay on the ground or had been burnt, and in a gap a broken cart stood jammed into the hedge. . . . . I might have left the place quite discontented even with mankind had I not recollected that the world is to the young, and noted that the children's diligence had been rewarded, and that one was handing something to the other with quite an air of pride" (169, 173).

In the same volume, "Salvagia," too, takes up the anti-Kailyard theme, emphasizing again the grim bleakness of rural life in Scotland. These pieces show that Graham's notation of the base, squalid detail was often tactical—as a deliberate riposte to sentimentalists. And in both "A Survival" and "Salvagia," Graham uses effectively his technique of "panorama terminating in close-up," in which a general survey is given final point and focus by a closely observed image or incident—perhaps a brief meeting and exchange of dialogue.

The three best pieces in *The Ipané* are probably "Un Angelito," "S.S. *Atlas*," and "Heather Jock." All three are strongly autobiographical: in each case Graham is recording with careful accumulation of detail some episode of his past life, nearly thirty years before the time of writing. Yet these are rather more than realistic evocations of an eventful past: there is a marked interest in the tellingly incongruous juxtaposition, and a preoccupation with the power of the sensuous memory to triumph over time. "Un Angelito," for instance, describes the occasion in Argentina in the 1870s when Graham and his fellow herdsmen attended a wake or *velorio:* a dance superintended by the seated corpse of a child, already "greenish in colour"; the crowds dance to a rasping guitar, while a man wounded by Indians lies nearby, smoking and eating chunks of beef to restore his strength. Finally, from the present time, Graham looks back on the distant scene:

In this monotony of mud and stucco, through the noise of cabs, of railways and the multitudinous sounds which rob the dweller in a city of any power of hearing, such as wild people have, I sometimes see my "Angelito" seated in his chair, and wonder in what kind of heaven he is. Often I have assisted at a "velorio," and done my best to honour the return of some small angel to his native land. Yet this first occasion on the Tres Arroyos still remains most firmly printed in my mind. Eustaquio Medina, the wounded man lying smoking on his catre, the decomposing "Angelito" in his chair, his mother looking at nothing with her eyes wide open, and the wild music of the cracked guitar seem to revisit me.

Lastly, the Pampa stretching away like a great inland sea, silent and bluish under the southern stars; and rising from it, the mysterious noises of the desert which, heard and comprehended, appeal to us in the same fashion as the instinct calling them north or south, stirs migratory birds.
(66–67)

In "S.S. *Atlas*" the incongruous associations of memory are again celebrated. Graham evokes, with a vividness which delighted Conrad, a stormy transatlantic crossing he had made in youth when the Scottish crew of the steamer had become so drunk at Hogmanay that the passengers had to man the ship. On that stormy voyage Graham had attempted to read the poetry of Edmund Spenser, with the result that now, whenever he opens the stained volume, "even the music of 'Epithalamion' is dumb, and in its stead I hear the swishing of the sea, feel the screw racing and the long-drawn-out notes of a 'forebitter' seem to quiver in the air, until I shut the book" (120).

The most incongruous juxtaposition in *The Ipané,* and a most complex demonstration of the associative memory, comes in "Heather Jock," in which Graham describes an old eccentric, a half-mad tramp and singer, who wandered the West of Scotland. Graham had been told of his death by a scrap of newspaper enclosed with a letter—a letter brought to Graham in Tucumán by a messenger who had just been pursued by Indians and whose brother had been killed by them in the chase. "At the fandango after the funeral, during the hot night, and whilst the fireflies flickered amongst the feathery tacuarás . . . . . I seemed to hear the jangling of the dead fool's bells, and listen to the minstrelsy, such as it was, of the hegemonist of Bridge of Weir" (186–87). The murdered Argentinian messenger; the dead Scottish hobo. The two men are linked only by a scrap of paper and one man's memory; and the significance, if any, is left to the reader to find: because after initial reflections, the narrator has stilled the voice of speculation—"for that way exegesis lies."

Thirteen Stories. Encouraged by the predominantly favorable reviews of *The Ipané,* in the following year Cunninghame Graham published a further collection of tales and sketches, *Thirteen Stories* (Heinemann, 1900). Here two of the items, "Rothenberger's Wedding" and "La Clemenza de Tito," deal boldly with sexual hypocrisy and male chauvinism; "Sohail" is a meditation on the flux and reflux of the Mohammedan empire; "In a German Tramp" contrasts the characters of a rough, sentimental German sea-captain and a dour but soft-hearted Scottish missionary; and "Sidi bu Zibbala" deals with a cosmopolitan eccentric who, after long travels, has concluded that all the world is not a stage but a dunghill, and accordingly takes up residence on a large dunghill in Morocco. "A Pakeha" and

"Higginson's Dream" sound the familiar theme of despoliation in the name of colonization, while the indictment of man's cruelty to animals is continued in "Calvary," a sketch that Shaw particularly admired; and Graham's reminiscences of his American adventures are resumed in "Cruz Alta," "A Hegira," and "La Pulperia."

In this volume Cunninghame Graham displays increasing technical proficiency: he experiments with oblique narrative forms and tales told in various vernaculars, as when, in "A Pakeha," the antiimperialistic point of the narrative lurks within the heavy Scottish brogue of the narrator, Mr. Campbell. There is no doubt that Graham was becoming more self-aware as a technician: when Garnett complained that the opening of "Victory" was prolix, Graham replied: "I wanted a heavy background . . . . . I am not a story teller, but an impressionist."[15] As it happens, "Victory" is unsuccessful, largely because in this sketch dealing with the Spanish-American War Graham's pro-Spanish sympathies are too sentimentally evident (the old Hispanic gentleman being so obviously noble, the Yankees so obviously coarse). A more controlled, more "finished" piece is "The Gold Fish," the tale of the Arab messenger who has to carry a bowl of goldfish across the Sahara from Rabat to the Sultan at Tafilet: after many miles he loses his way and eventually dies of thirst, while beside him the glass bowl glints unbroken in the desert sun. This memorable tale, at once an evocation of fidelity and futility, of endurance and absurdity, rightly became one of Graham's most celebrated pieces, appearing in numerous anthologies.

Garnett claimed that Graham was "more than fifty years ahead of his time,"[16] and the tale "A Hegira" proves this claim by virtue of the narrator's sympathy with the Indian fugitives in Mexico and his depiction of the racial arrogance and callousness of the Texan cowboy who helps to kill them (while sparing, in response to an appeal from his concubine, their dog). "Wal," the Texan remarks, "we had to bury them, for dead Injun stinks worse than turkey-buzzard, and the dodgasted little dog is sitting on the grave, 'pears like he's froze, leastwise he hasn't moved since sun-up, when we planted the whole crew" (142). Graham, who had traveled the "wild west" when it *was* wild, is from his own experience offering here a critical anticipation of the type that Hollywood would later, for many years, idealize and glamorize. Not until the late 1960s and the 1970s did the cinema, in films like *Little Big Man* and *Soldier Blue,* give fair consideration to the claim that Graham often made:

that the Indians should be seen as the patriots and the white men as the arrogant (and sometimes genocidal) invaders.

Graham was also ahead of his time by virtue of his support of the feminist movement, and "Rothenberger's Wedding" indicates this allegiance. Rothenberger is depicted as a complacent, successful German physician who provides electrical therapy for the rheumatic and gouty; "his literary taste bounded by idealistic novels about materialistic folk, and the drum-taps of the bards of Anglo-Saxon militarism; the doctor looked on the world as a vast operating theatre, sparing not even his own foibles in his diagnosis of mankind. All sentiment he held if not accursed, yet as superfluous." Furthermore: "Women he held inferior to men, as really do almost all men, although they fear to say so . . . . ." In London he prospers but feels that to be accorded the full accolade of respectability he needs a wife—"a 'real legitimate,' to prove to all his patients that he was a moral man." He courts a well-to-do girl from Hampstead and proceeds to the wedding. The night before it, at a hotel, he had felt himself falling in love with a chamber-maid there; and after the ceremony, when changing in the hotel room, he meets the chamber-maid again and, it is implied, copulates with her, while the bride, her father, and the bridesmaids wait down below. He concludes: " 'Marriage is good for a man, it sober him, it bring him business, and it bring him children, and . . . I am happy mit my wife. . . . The housemaid, oh yes, ach Got[t], I hear that some one take from the place to live mit him, and it is not a wonder, for she was so tall, so stout, have such black hair, and such great eyes, it was a pity that she spend her life answering the bell, and bringing up hot water in a jug' " (226). The sense that the German thinks lingeringly and longingly of the maid, the sense that he is aware, after all, that he has paid an emotional price for his success, checks the tendency of this tale toward satiric caricature, even though a suggestion of patronizing caricature is certainly conveyed by Graham's use of a stage-comedian's German accent (" 'mein wife mit the bridesmaids . . . . . .' ").

A tougher, more adroit tale is the next one, "La Clemenza de Tito." Here the narrator reports a meeting with a much-traveled old seaman who had once visited a black prostitute at Perim. As she undressed, the seaman was shocked to see that she wore a crucifix:

"[R]ound her black neck she had a silver crucifix, contrast of colour made
the thing stand out double the size. Ses I, 'What's that?' and she says,
'Klistian girl, Johnny, me Klistian all the same you.' That was a stopper
over all, and I just reached for my hat, says, 'Klistian are yer,' and I gave
her two of them Spanish dollars and a kiss, and quit the place. What did
she say? Why, nothing, looked at me and laughed, and says, 'You Klistian,
Johnny, plenty much damn fool.' No, I don't know what she meant
. . . . ." (233)

And the seaman goes, leaving the narrator and the reader to consider
the widening ironies of this brief anecdote.

Perhaps the most richly satisfying of all the pieces in *Thirteen
Stories,* though, is the first, "Cruz Alta": the long reminiscence of
Graham's early attempt with Mansel to make a fortune by driving
that herd of horses from Uruguay into Brazil. Over hill, across river,
through jungle they trekked, only to find on arrival that they would
be lucky to sell the animals at any price. It is keenly evocative of
people and places; of Xavier Fernández, for example, the retired
slave-dealer in his old straw hat, bed-ticking trousers, and with
naked feet shoved into slippers of carpincho leather, riding his mule;
or of the drunken Dutchman who entertained Graham to dinner in
a room inhabited by pigs, a half-grown tapir, and two new-caught
screaming macaws. This is the tale in which Graham presents most
forthrightly the philosophy which was to earn him the reputation
of "The Apostle of Failure." He writes:

> Failure alone is interesting . . . . .
> [T]hose who fail after a glorious fashion, Raleigh, Cervantes, Chatter-
> ton, Camoens, Blake, Claverhouse, Lovelace, Alcibiades, Parnell, and the
> last unknown deck-hand who, diving overboard after a comrade, sinks
> without saving him: these interest us, at least they interest those who,
> cursed with imagination, are thereby doomed themselves to the same
> failure as their heroes were. The world is to the unimaginative, for them
> are honours, titles, rank and ample waistbands; foolish phylacteries broad
> as trade union banners; their own esteem and death to sound of Bible
> leaves fluttered by sorrowing friends, with the sure hope of waking up
> immortal in a new world on the same pattern as the world that they have
> left. (6–7)

Now this notion of "the success of failure" has various sources.
Christianity has long taught that worldly success is an impediment
to salvation; and the Romantic movement propagated the idea that

the noble person is one who is doomed to suffer. The Aesthetic Movement of the 1890s, which nurtured paradox and the desire to *épater le bourgeois,* has left its mark; and there is also a clear element of self-justification (even of self-congratulation) for the Graham of Gartmore, the uncrowned king with a heavily mortgaged estate whose commercial ventures had a habit of failing. To the muddled thought of the old paradox, however, Graham brought a new, rash vigor of expression; he repeated it in numerous works; and that tag, "The Apostle of Failure," stuck to him for a long time.

But of course the value of "Cruz Alta" lies not in its pretensions to philosophy but in its vivid remembrance of the places and people—and horses—encountered by Graham on that far-off South American odyssey. The nostalgia is tempered by the wry humor and the mundane detail:

Fastening our horses to long twisted green-hide ropes, we passed into the house. "Carne con cuero" (meat cooked with the hide) was roasting near the front-door on a great fire of bones. Around it men sat drinking maté, smoking and talking, whilst tame ostriches peered into the fire and snapped up anything within their reach; dogs without hair, looking like pigs, ran to and fro, horses were tied to every post, fire-flies darted about the trees; and above all, the notes, sung in a high falsetto voice of a most lamentable Paraguayan "triste," quavered in the night air and set the dogs a-barking, when all the company at stated intervals took up the refrain, and chanted hoarsely or shrilly of the hardships passed by Lopez in his great camp at Pirayú. (15–16)

At the subsequent dance, Graham found that custom obliged him to present a handkerchief to his partner. "I having a bad cold saw with regret my new silk handkerchief pass to the hand of a mulatto girl, and having asked her for her own as a remembrance of her beauty and herself, received a home-made cotton cloth, stiff as a piece of leather, and with meshes like a sack" (17). Such closeness of notation may remind us of the character in a later tale who praises James Boswell for having "an eye untill him like a corbie [crow] for detail" and remarks: "Details, ye ken, are just the vertebrae of the world." This was evidently Cunninghame Graham's view: he claimed that "The small things of life in sum total work out greater than the larger matters, which at first sight seem so important."[17]

Retrospect. Looking back over the tales and sketches of the early period, then, we can see that Graham soon developed a dis-

tinctive proficiency in his chosen literary *genres*. If slight, they had
the tang of knowledgeable authenticity. Although opinionative, his
views were radical and provocative, and they were balanced by a
realist's determination to present life with scrupulous accuracy.
There came gradually some curbing of his faults, chronic though
they were: these being a rather diffuse or erratic presentation, the
narrative being too readily sidetracked by digression; the tendency
to offer prolix descriptive catalogs; and the occasionally unreliable
grammar, syntax, and punctuation. Graham was an oral and aural
sensualist: he relished the tang and flavor that exotic phrases gave
to a description, and was fond—sometimes overfond—of displaying
Spanish lore and phraseology: "Horses went better, 'maté' was hotter
in the mouth, the pulperia caña seemed more tolerable, and the
'China' girls looked more desirable than usual . . . . . I arrived
upon a 'pingo' . . . . . or on a 'mancaron' " (*TS*, 8–9). Such
displays may tempt a parodist, and Stephen Graham, in *The Death
of Yesterday*,[18] readily succumbed to the temptation by offering a
passage which most evidently parodies "Cruz Alta": "It was fine
over there, *gauchos, estancias, potreros, sanchochos, Chinas*, singing
cielitos on the *gato*, mounted on *agenos*, eating *carne con cuero*, dancing
the *pericon* . . . . ."

Literary critics have given insufficient attention to the fact that
faults may be merits. More precisely: there are particular contexts
in which apparent defects may in some measure be assets. If, for
example, a work is or purports to be autobiographical, and if the
autobiographer, as presented to us, is no professional writer or
novelist but, say, a man of action, then a certain ruggedness, awk-
wardness, or clumsiness of style and a certain vagrancy of narrative
sequence may actually enhance our sense of the reality of the narrator
and his world. In Defoe's *Robinson Crusoe*, the style has a practical
directness, rather than grace or elegance or sensitivity, and some
of the narrative episodes (e.g., the building of the unlaunchable
boat) seem to lead nowhere. But because the ostensible narrator is
not a Henry James or a Flaubert but one "Robinson Crusoe, of
York, Mariner"—a seaman and merchant-venturer and castaway—
the apparent gracelessness helps to generate a powerful authenticity.
In Graham's case, some of the lapses that may irritate can also seem
appropriate to the character of a man of action turned late to writing.
He could be very self-aware and even too "literary"; he could be

casual and slapdash; but between the two extremes his work, with its mixture of qualities, can evoke his personality very effectively. In 1900, surveying the reviews of his collections of tales, Graham could feel satisfied that he had firmly established his literary reputation. A few reviewers had recoiled, but the majority applauded the work. Sometimes there were complaints about Graham's sexual boldness ("very strong meat") and ruthless realism: a reviewer in the *Spectator* said, for example, "Some of his descriptions are perhaps a little too realistic; one, of the body of a woman killed by Indians and hung to a post, is almost revolting, and might well have been spared. . . . . Readers who object to a spade being called a spade had better look elsewhere for their entertainment." The offending passage, which actually has a Conradian quality of black irony, was from "Un Angelito": "We had seen a woman's body hanging naked to a post, and decorated with leaves torn from a Bible skewered artistically about it where decency required" (*Ipané*, 55). Sometimes there were complaints about his profuse opinionativeness: "Its faults are on the side of a crowding of ideas and vehemence of expression," said a reviewer of *Thirteen Stories* in the periodical *Literature,* while a sharper thrust came from the *Academy*'s reviewer of *The Ipané:* "There is nothing more conventional than the hatred of conventionality." But on the whole, the majority of those early reviews were distinctly gratifying. "Vivid descriptive powers," "a cynic touch which will please the literary student," "exquisite skill" (*Literature*); "There is nothing better than the pleasure of talking with an honest man who knows the world and has measured the value of failure and success" (*Speaker*); "one of the wittiest commentators on civilisation, imperialism, and the trading spirit in our midst" (*Academy*). "He is a literary impressionist, who with a few bold strokes vivifies the dry bones of fleeting memories. . . . . His cynicism has much of the pungency of Voltaire. . . . . Many heresies may be forgiven or at least ignored for the sake of brilliant individuality in a humdrum age. . . . . Every page is instinct with grace and beauty" (*Saturday Review*).[19]

The reviewer's reference to the "literary impressionist" is a reminder of an obvious and potent influence on Graham. In 1895 the *Review of Reviews* remarked: "Impressionism would seem to be 'the new thing' in fiction."[20] The paintings of Manet, Monet, and their fellow artists had stressed the value of the glimpse, the fleeting moment, the apparently accidental; they had demoted the narrative, moralistic, and posed aspects of traditional painting. The resultant interest encouraged writers to offer vivid glimpses: telling moments of life rather than rationally elaborated narratives. And for such pieces of "literary impressionism" there was an ample market: in the 1890s an abundance of periodicals provided generous space for literary features: Graham read Conrad's African tales in *Blackwood's* and *Cosmopolis,* while his own pieces were given hospitality in the *Saturday Reveiw* and the *Nineteenth Century,* for example.

Other influences on his work were soon noted by the reviewers. Some mentioned that he was a rival to Kipling. Others saw the resemblance to Maupassant, who offered a model for the coolly ironic treatment of the hypocrisies and brutalities of bourgeois and neasant, and a precedent for the frank presentation of whores. Certainly the Frenchman's philosophical skepticism left its mark. Graham's early pamphlet *The Imperial Kailyard* observes: "Principles, Maupassant has justly said, are by their very nature false and sterile. Are they not ideas reputed fixed and immutable? Fixed and immutable ideas in a world where all is changing, where light is an illusion, where sound is an illusion of our senses" (5). Edward Garnett (whose wife, Constance, was busily translating into English all the great Russian novelists) introduced Graham to Turgenev's work, and *A Sportsman's Sketches,* with their blend of romantic melancholy and observant humanity, he soon ranked alongside Maupassant's tales. In the role of benign spirits rather than literary influences were Chaucer and, of course, Cervantes. Chaucer, the early master of the drily ironic character study, delighted him. Cervantes's preoccupation with the tragicomic interplay of Quixotic idealism and Sanchesque realism, with the incongruities of romantic aspiration in a base world, and indeed the very fact that Cervantes turned late to writing after being battered and bruised in a life of action: all this made him a tutelary deity to Graham's imagination.

Inevitably, comparison with such august literary predecessors emphasizes the slapdash, egoistic, and clumsy aspects of Cunninghame Graham's output, but if we treat him as a writer in a predominantly autobiographical mode we will be able to appreciate his limited but distinct achievements.

Mogreb-el-Acksa.   The collections of tales included many memorable pieces—"Cruz Alta," "The Gold Fish," and "A Jesuit" among them—but, in the eyes of many critics, Graham's major work in this early period was the travel book *Mogreb-el-Acksa,* 1898.

(He translates the title as "The Far West".) This tells of Graham's abortive journey across Morocco in autumn 1897, when he had attempted, disguised as an Arab sheikh or sherif (Mohammed el Fasi), to reach the "Forbidden City" of Tarudant in the Atlas Mountains and had been arrested by the Kaid of Kintafi and held prisoner at the Kaid's fortress high above the rocky pass.

This is the book that made Conrad stamp gleefully about his house: he said, "No thirsty men drank water as we have been drinking in, swallowing, tasting, blessing, enjoying gurgling, choking over, absorbing, your thought, your phrases, your irony, the spirit of your vision and of Your expression. The individuality of the book is amazing—even to me who know you or pretend to. It is wealth tossed on the roadside, it is a creative achievement, it is alive with conviction and truth." If not quite as enthusiastic as Conrad, the reviewers were generally enthusiastic about *Mogreb,* which subsequently Paul Bloomfield termed "a masterpiece" and Richard Haymaker called "a minor masterpiece of travel literature."[21]

Mogreb arises from that long, exotic tradition of the nineteenth century which had its culmination in the twentieth: the tradition of those European gentlemen who, with a mixture of motives (romantic or practical, led by love of adventure or gain or by curiosity), explored Arabia, often disguising themselves as Arabs to facilitate their journeys. These explorers included John L. Burckhardt, Sir Richard Burton, Gifford Palgrave, Charles Huber, Friedrich Rohlfs, C. M. Doughty, and Wilfrid Scawen Blunt. Blunt, who was a friend of Graham's, was an enthusiastic admirer of Arabian culture: he translated Arabic texts into English, brought Arab horses to England to form the renowned Crabbet stud, and nurtured ambitions of helping the Arabs to repulse the Turks. Graham helped to link the newer and the older generations of Arabists when he introduced T. E. Lawrence to Blunt. Lawrence met the veteran traveler at Newbuildings in Sussex, Blunt's ancient house hung with Moorish tapestries: "There in a great chair he sat . . . . . like a careless work of art in well-worn Arab robes, his chiselled face framed in silvered, curling hair . . . . . Blunt was a fire yet flickering over the ashes of old fury."[22] The "fury" was, in part, his antiimperialistic fervor: he had long been a bitter critic of British colonial policy, and this was another matter in which Graham sympathized with him.

Even without Blunt's example, however, there is no doubt that
Graham's love of risky traveling, his taste for cultural confrontations,
and his yearning for hot, exotic lands would eventually have led
him to Morocco. In winter 1894 he visited the country with the
young artist William Rothenstein, delighting in his encounters with
the Arabs and attempting to impress them with his pistol-shooting
and feats of dexterity with a long rifle. And in 1897 he again set
out for Morocco, this time initially alone. His ostensible aim was
to reach the "Forbidden City" of Tarudant in the Sus region, amid
the Atlas Mountains: "the only Moorish city to which an air of
mystery clings," in a province "of vines, or orange gardens, olive
yards, plantations of pomegranates, Roman remains, rich mines"
(*Mogreb*, 2). Apart from the traditional antipathy between Muslim
and Christian, what made Tarudant "Forbidden" was that the Sultan
of Morocco, aware that European traders were casting avaricious eyes
on the region, had banned them from the Sus. Even while Graham
was in the country, Major Spilsbury (an acquaintance of his), agent
for the London-based Globe Venture Syndicate, had attempted to
smuggle guns to some of the tribesmen of the South but had been
chased away by the Sultan's troops and a gunboat. The chieftains
were on the alert; and that is the main reason why the story unfolded
in *Mogreb* is the story of yet another failure for Cunninghame
Graham.

Mogreb tells how Graham first arrived at Tangier and voyaged
down the western coast to disembark at Mogador. The coastal route
ahead was closed, as the Howara tribe was in rebellion: Graham
would have to follow a longer and mountainous inland route. As
companions in the venture, he hired a Syrian, Hassan Lutaif; a
Moor, Haj Mohammed es Swani; and as guide there was a Berber,
Mohammed el Hosein. A muleteer, Ali, joined them, being reluc-
tant to lose sight of the mules he had hired to the party. Graham
shaved his own head, donned white robes, a turban and a blue cloak;
and, after considering various roles, chose to become "Mohammed
el Fasi," a Sheikh or Sherif, a physician and holy man. On the
journey he gravely dispensed his blessings, prescribed medicines for
ophthalmic patients, and divided Seidlitz powders into small por-
tions "to be taken at stated times to serve as aphrodisiacs." On
horseback Graham rode proudly through the throng at a village
market, "not even looking down when the poor fellows lifted [his]
cloak and kissed the hem." Higher and higher into the mountains

the conspiratorial group struggled on, over narrow, rugged tracks, pitching their tents at night.

A setback, probably a crucial one, came when Graham found that his horse had a fistulous sore: he bargained for another steed with a Shillah tribesman who may have sent ahead his suspicions about the true nationality of "Sheikh Mohammed." Passing a hill, the travelers sighted an immense castle surrounded by gardens and woods, with the river El N'fiss rushing beneath the walls: this was Talet el Jacub, the stronghold of the Kaid (or Caid) of Kintafi, governor of the province. A messenger from the castle came and questioned them, saying that there were rumors that a Christian disguised as a Mohammedan was on the road. Reassured by their replies, the messenger apologized and returned; Graham's band rejoiced, for now there seemed no further dangers: in a few hours they would be able to look down on the gleaming minarets of the mosques of Tarudant. Suddenly a party of men brandishing guns ran from the castle, seized the travelers, and hustled them inside. A chamberlain announced that they were now the guests of the Kaid and must await his pleasure—in a leaky tent pitched for the "guests" on waterlogged ground, under the angry eyes of the many people in the courtyard.

And there, on meager rations, they were held captive for day after day. Their lot was not as unpleasant as that of the gang of convicts who, after laboring in the daytime, were at night lowered into a stinking pit which was then covered over with a stone until dawn. Yet Graham's situation was ludicrous, anxious, and depressing, he having come so near his goal and being now so far from it. Gradually he became immured to the life and came even to enjoy the setting, with icy mountain-peaks around and the river splashing below, and the strange company of travelers at the fort. There was a Negro with silver earring and tattooed cheek who had worked for the doomed Cape Juby Company on the coast. There was a wandering minstrel who knew Paris, Vienna, Budapest, Tripoli, Cairo, and Turkey. There were three Kaids who had already been camping for a month, awaiting an audience with the lord of the stronghold; while another suppliant, ragged and famine-stricken, had waited six months in the courtyard.

At long last it was Graham's turn to be received by the Kaid in his presence-chamber, where, at either side of their lord, "Two negro boys with dirty handkerchiefs, and boughs of walnut, stood

. . . . . and flapped away the flies." It was a doubly incongruous meeting: on the one side a stern Berber chieftain, puzzled by the stranger's motives, and striving to maintain the courteous fiction that the captive was a guest; on the other side, a Scottish skeptic, taken to be an English Christian, still wearing the now-useless disguise of a Muslim holy man. As though in a modern version of the legends of the Grail Quester and the maimed Fisher King, the Kaid bore a wound in the thigh (caused by a musket-ball in a recent skirmish); and there were hints that Graham might attempt surgery on the wound—a possibility that the Scot prudently declined. Although elaborate courtesies were maintained throughout the audience, it was clear that the Kaid would not permit Graham to travel on to Tarudant.

Meanwhile, Graham had bribed a *rekass,* a runner, to carry a smuggled mesage from the captives to a missionary at Mogador. "On the evening of the third day from that on which he went, a dusty little man knocked at the missionary's door more than a hundred miles away" and handed over the message. The missionary contacted the British authorities; diplomacy was exerted; and on the morning of 30 October, after twelve days of detention, Graham was ejected from the castle. He made one final request to be allowed to proceed to Tarudant, but was told by the Chamberlain that this was a grave question if he thought he had the best horse in the valley and if, "supposing any tribesman was to fire by accident," Graham deemed his robes thick enough to deflect the ball. Wearily, Graham returned to Mogador.

A year later, the story of the failed journey was published by Heinemann; and the loyal Edward Garnett led the reviewers' tributes to the book. In the *Academy,* he described *Mogreb-el-Acksa* as "a delicious commentary on our Anglo-Saxon civilisation; a malicious and ironic comparison of [the] British commercialised world with the feudal world of Morocco; a subtle, witty commentary that must rejoice all who are rejoiced by Candide."[23] As always in Graham's work, however, there are flaws. The narrative has a digressive copiousness, and greater selectivity would have helped; and there is carelessness in the presentation, with repetitions of fact and the customary slips in grammar and even spelling. These flaws do little to diminish the sense of the energetic, incisive richness of the book. There are numerous vivid descriptive cameos of people and places, their proportion increasing toward the end; many figures appear briefly but stamp themselves on the memory: the officious, sly, but honest chamberlain, for example; the runner who zealously carried the smuggled message; and the Tunisian doctor in red fez encountered on the boat: "Though not a linguist, still a competent practitioner, trepanning people's heads with ease, and putting in pieces of gourd instead of silver as being lighter . . . . . Qunine he had, and blistering fluid, with calomel and other simples, and when the Christian quinine ran out, he made more for himself out of the ashes of an oleander stick mixed with burnt scales of fish and dead men's bones, and found his preparation, which he styled 'El quina beladia' (native-made quinine), even more efficacious than the drug from over sea. . . . ." (17–18).

Another cameo is that of the poor petitioner who for six months had been seeking the Kaid's help:

Meantime the man slept in the mosque by night, by day stood at the gate, and when the Caid rode out clung to his stirrup and implored his aid. He said, "I see him every six or seven days, but there is no hope but in God." Still he was cheerful, and had his rags well washed; and was as resigned and dignified as I am certain that no Christian, out of fiction, could possibly have been. "God the great Helper"; but then how slow but merciful in this case, if only by the faith he had implanted to endure his own neglect. And so the sad-hearted man of sorrows made his notch upon my life, as the old Persian and the "Oudad" had done, and still perhaps waits for the Caid on mornings when his Excellency rides out to hunt or hawk with a long train of followers, issuing from the horse-shoe arch, with negroes holding greyhounds in the leash, horsemen perched high on their red saddles, the sun falling upon long silver-mounted guns. . . . . (254–55)

These two passages convey Graham's ability to evoke rapidly, inelegantly perhaps but proficiently, the odd and absurd, the poignant and the picturesque. In the latter quotation, the pessimistic religious irony about "God the great Helper" is one of many such observations which give a recurrent tone of philosophical melancholy. The central force of *Mogreb*, as Garnett rightly saw, is to be found not only in its evocative skill but also in its vigorous questioning of the presuppositions of Victorian England and imperialistic Europe. Graham does not mince his words.

But as I see the matter Europeans are a curse throughout the East. What do they bring worth bringing, as a general rule?

Guns, gin, powder, and shoddy cloths, dishonest dealing only too frequently, and flimsy manufactures which displace the fabrics woven by the women, new wants, new ways, and discontent with what they know, and no attempt to teach a proper comprehension of what they introduce; these are the blessings Europeans take to Eastern lands. (24–25)

To recapture the iconoclastic force of such words, we need only recall that in the year of *Mogreb*'s publication, 1898, the Conservative prime minister, Lord Salisbury, had said, "From the necessities of politics or under the pretence of philanthropy—the living nations will gradually encroach on the territory of the dying. . . . . We shall not allow England to be at a disadvantage in any re-arrangement."[24]

Mogreb challenges comparison with the classics of Victorian travel-writing: with, for example, A. W. Kinglake's *Eothen*, Sir Richard Burton's *Pilgrimage to Al-Madinah and Meccah*, and C. M. Doughty's *Arabia Deserta*. Granted, these other writers were far longer afield than Graham; all had more detailed and intimate knowledge of things Arabian and Oriental; all had more spectacular adventures. Kinglake's account of his tribulations during the plague at Cairo is still gripping to read, and his famous description of the Sphynx, although now obtrusively "literary" in its self-conscious rhetoric, still has interest as a passage heralding Walter Pater (the description of the Mona Lisa in *The Renaissance*) and the Aesthetes. Burton's *Pilgrimage* is animate with the intrepid strength and arrogance of this man who dared to shoulder the true pilgrims out of the way to gain sight of the sacred stone at Mecca. And Doughty's is the narrative of a man who risked death, took hard knocks, and knew humiliation, but compiled an encyclopedic stock of Eastern lore and wrought an artificially archaic but often expressive style for its communication. Yet, although Graham lacks their range of knowl-edge and incident, although he had no belletristic elegance, his work stands the test well. The quick responsiveness, the enquiring intelligence, the satiric edge, the undercurrents of stoic melancholy, and the readiness to probe beneath cultural appearances—these am-ply sustain it.

Graham was "ahead of his times," but not divorced from his age. He struggled boldly with many of the prejudices of his day, but some of them were within him as well as outside him. The resultant tensions give much of *Mogreb* a quality of cultural paradox. He stresses that Arabs are best left untrammeled by European ways, having more freedom and dignity now than they could have if their land were Europeanized; but when he is describing Jews (several of whom treated him cordially and hospitably on his journey) a familiar cluster of anti-Semitic notions—that Jews are conspiratorial, manipulative, avaricious, and generally unsavory—hovers nearby, and when he does concede that a particular Jew is a worthy person, the tone is sometimes rather patronizing. Another feature which time has made more prominent is the vanity of Graham's attitude. Although traveling a foreign region without permission or authority, and in disguise, and although promptly and rightly arrested, Graham still expects to be treated as a British gentleman and is gratified when his captor supplies an additional tent so that he may sleep apart from his lesser attendants and with only his personal servant, Lutaif, at hand. But even as this last criticism is being made it transforms itself into praise. For part of the fascination of *Mogreb* lies in its record of a proud personality embarking on an odyssey which is both romantic and ludicrous: and Graham is often able to see what is comical in his own plight, the plight of an atheistical Scottish laird arrested while posing as an Islamic doctor and holy man. "I . . . . . wondered if an English Duke in the Georgian times would have treated an Arab wandering in England, and giving out he was an English clergyman, as well as the wild, semi-independent Berber Sheikh treated the wandering Englishman who assumed to pass, not merely as a clergyman, but as a saint" (245).

Another of the ironic tensions of the book is between Graham the radical primitivist, who strives to argue that for all its poverty, life under the Moroccan sun is better for the people than life in the gray industrial countries, and Graham the pessimistic realist, who sees the wretchedness of the Moroccan poor and whose nose reminds him that "in the air, above the scent of flowers, hung the stench of human excrement" (134). He conveys the vitality of Morocco, but he also flinches in distaste from the Reckitt's blue and the gilding of the presence-chamber and notes with pity the infected eyes of famished children.

The classics of Victorian travel literature were once widely known and were often to be encountered in schools and universities: *Eothen* was a very popular school text in England in the 1940s. But now the genre is neglected. One reason is obvious. In days of cheap air travel, when millions of people can annually travel the world for their holidays, the need for vicarious travel (into the Orient—and into the past—in the company of Kinglake and the others) declines; and the easy imagery of television and the cinema obscures the subtler imagery of those writers' descriptive passages. But in the foregoing discussion, we have noted that there is at least one text of that genre—*Mogreb-el-Acksa*—which deserves reconsideration; and not only on the grounds of its descriptive panache, but also because it richly embodies some of the most interesting cultural tensions and paradoxes of its era.

The paradoxes are augmented by a recent discovery. In the text, as we have seen, Graham stresses that his motive for traveling the region was mere curiosity, and he inveighs against European traders who attempt to bring commerce and an alien culture to the Moroccan people. Yet among his papers I have found a document in Arabic, of which the translation begins: "Let it be known to the reader of this that I the undersigned, Sheikh el-Bashir Ben Sheikh Mohammed Ben Beyrouk, Chief and headman of Tiris and all the surrounding district, do hereby agree and covenant to give to . . . . . Robert Cunninghame Graham, the Englishman, and Najib Kisbany, the Syrian, the exclusive right of trading in the above mentioned Country in all kind of goods and products both import and export and of searching for and working minerals . . . . ."[25] Tiris is in the Río de Oro region to the south of Morocco. The correspondence shows that, from 1898 ónward, Graham pursued intermittently for some years the possibility of forming a company or syndicate to trade there. The venture was, perhaps fortunately, another abortive one.

In 1963, when working in Graham's study at Ardoch, I took down from the bookshelves the copy of Shaw's *Three Plays for Puritans* that the author had presented to his Scottish friend; and inside was the following inscription in ink: "to Mr. R.B.C.G., the onlie begetter of Captain Brassbound, from G. Bernard Shaw. Jan. 1901." This dedication, echoing Shakespeare's dedication of his sonnets, is explained in Shaw's notes to *Captain Brassbound's Conversion,* which begin: "I claim as a notable merit in the authorship of this play that I have been intelligent enough to steal its scenery, its surroundings, its atmosphere, its geography, its knowledge of the east, its fascinating Cadis and Krooboys and Sheikhs and mud castles from an excellent book of philosophic travel and vivid adventure entitled Mogreb-el-Acksa. . . . ."[26] Shaw does not mention that he had supplemented his borrowings from the book by sending to Cunninghame Graham a long questionnaire on points of detail, ranging from matters of pronunciation ("How do you pronounce Sheikh? Is it Shike?") to the dress of a missionary and even to the fee charged by a guide. Graham's answers ran to nearly five pages, and almost all were incorporated into the play, either in the dialogue or the directions.[27] So to Cunninghame Graham, Shaw's comedy owes not only the basic setting and situation (Europeans held captive in the Atlas Mountains) but also a wealth of local knowledge.

In the notes to the play, Shaw repaid the debt by praising *Mogreb* and providing a witty pen-portrait of Graham, of whom he says:

He is, I understand, a Spanish hidalgo: hence the superbity of his portrait by Lavery (Velasquez being no longer available). He is, I know, a Scotch laird. How he contrives to be authentically the two things at the same time is no more intelligible to me than the fact that everything that has ever happened to him seems to have happened in Paraguay or Texas instead of in Spain or Scotland. He is, I regret to add, an impenitent and unashamed dandy: such boots, such a hat, would have dazzled D'Orsay himself. With that hat he once saluted me in Regent St. when I was walking with my mother. Her interest was instantly kindled; and the following conversation ensued. "Who is that?" "Cunninghame Graham." "Nonsense! Cunninghame Graham is one of your Socialists: that man is a gentleman."[28]

Chapter Three
The Histories
A Vanished Arcadia

Without doubt, Cunninghame Graham's most richly fruitful period as an author was from 1898 to 1901. In that short time he published not only two lively collections of short pieces and the best of his travel books (*Mogreb*), but also the first and best of his histories, a volume that continues to be cited from time to time in the long controversy about the Jesuits in Paraguay.

The publication of this volume, *A Vanished Arcadia*, 1901, marked the start of his series of histories of the Spanish Conquest of South and Cental America. Subsequent volumes were: *Hernando de Soto*, 1903; *Bernal Díaz del Castillo*, 1915; *The Conquest of New Granada*, 1922; *The Conquest of the River Plate*, 1924; *Pedro de Valdivia*, 1926; and *The Horses of the Conquest*, 1930. There were numerous reasons for his embarking on this long project.

Cunninghame Graham, himself of Spanish ancestry (hence that nickname, "Don Roberto"), had since childhood cultivated an interest in Hispanic culture and history, and in his journeys in the Americas he had inevitably encountered the relics of the Conquest. As a romantic and man of action, he could well see the ostensibly glamorous aspects of the conquistadores' careers, their bravery and hardihood in battling against hostile terrain and enemies who outnumbered them. For Graham, a keen equestrian who was to dedicate one of his volumes to his horse, Pampa, the glamour was accentuated by the crucial role that horses had played in the Conquest, being creatures unknown and initially terrifying to the natives: *The Horses of the Conquest* would be a book devoted to this topic. Then from the first, his writings had been preoccupied with what, for a variable skeptic, was often the poignant tragicomedy of religious faith: the faith that drives men to conquest or to death; to triumph, to slaughter others, or to be slaughtered. He watched for the combination of proselytizing religion and material aggrandizement: imperialism both spiritual and territorial, a service perhaps of Mammon in the name of God. Temperamentally, he had far more sympathy with Catholicism than with Scottish Calvinism; it was appropriate that his wife should have been the biographer of Santa Teresa.

We can see that Graham's chivalric desire to defend the underdog was again important in the motivation of this series. This desire had many aspects. First, Graham believed that Hispanic (and especially Hispanic-American) culture was itself an underdog—an area neglected by Anglo-Saxon readers. Second, he considered the conquistadores to be the underdogs of history—or, certainly, of history as written by Anglo-Saxon historians: "It is an article of Anglo-Saxon faith that all the Spanish colonies were maladministered, and all the Spanish conquerors bloodthirsty butchers . . . . ." (*VA*, xi). He hoped to redress a balance by suggesting that the conquistadores were either not as villainous as they had been depicted or at least no worse than their modern counterparts.

Of course, his discussion of the Spanish Conquest was part of Graham's vast criticism of imperialism. If modern imperialists claimed to be enlightened bringers of progress and that the Spanish conquerors of old had been mere ruthless exploiters, he would strive to expose the claims as modern hypocrisy. In keeping with this aim, he gives particular attention to the relatively humane conquistadores; and, true to his defense of the underdog, he gives pride of place in his series not to the famous leaders, Cortés and Pizarro, but to the less celebrated ones, such as Valdivia and Núñez. Of course, what leads Graham repeatedly into moral entanglements in this series is that the most obvious underdogs in the whole conquest were the natives, who fought bravely but who again and again were vanquished, slaughtered, or enslaved by the Spaniards; and it is with them, ultimately, that Graham's mobile sympathies lie. This shifting balance of judgment, the way in which he now rides enthusiastically alongside Alvar Núñez or de Soto and now rejoices as a band of Indians defies the invaders, is one of the most interesting features of these histories. If Cunninghame Graham were more consistent, he would be far less engaging.

The first volume in the series, *A Vanished Arcadia,* is the richest and most ample. The Preface cites several of the causal factors that we have listed. The motive of nostalgia is frankly, indeed poignantly, admitted:

Wandering about the countries of which now I treat . . . . . I made no
notes of anything, caring most chiefly for the condition of my horse, yet
when I think on them, pampa and cordillera, virgin forest, the "passes"
of the rivers, approached by sandy paths, bordered by flowering and sweet-
smelling trees, and most of all the deserted Jesuit Missions, half buried
by the vigorous vegetation, and peopled but by a few white-clad Indians,
rise up so clearly that, without the smallest faculty for dealing with that
which I have undertaken, I am forced to write. Flowers, scents, the herds
of horses, the ostriches, and the whole charm of that New World which
those who saw it even a quarter of a century ago saw little altered from
the remotest times, have remained clear and sharp, and will remain so
with me to the end. (vii–viii)

Then there is the desire to defend the various underdogs: the underdog among subjects, Spanish South America, "a subject quite
fallen out of date"; and the Jesuits themselves, unjustly maligned
as Machiavels: "Your Jesuit is, as we know, the most tremendous
wild-fowl that the world has known. 'La guardia nera' of the Pope,
the order which has wrought so much destruction, the inventors
of 'La Ciencia media,' cradle from which has issued forth Molina,
Suarez, and all those villains who, in the day in which the doctrine
was unfashionable, decried mere faith, and took their stand on
works—who in this land of preconceived opinion can spare it a good
word?"(viii–ix).
    This prejudice against the Jesuit missions is an old one. In Vol-
taire's *Candide*, Cacambo says of the Jesuits in Paraguay: *Los padres
y ont tout, et les peuples rien; c'est le chef-d'œuvre de la raison et de la
justice* ("The priests there own everything, and the people nothing;
it's a triumph of reason and justice"). Graham also knew that Richard
F. Burton, in his *Letters from the Battlefields of Paraguay* (1870), had
reviled the Jesuits' system as a "theocratic despotism" which paved
the way for the modern era of dictatorships there. (To Englishmen,
the novelist Anthony Burgess remarked in 1980, "Jesuitry
. . . . . means militancy, fanaticism, equivocation, unscrupu-
lousness . . . . ."[1]) The Jesuits may have been reviled, but the
young Graham had encountered living testimony to the humanity
of their regimes in Paraguay: in 1873, in the deserted missions, he
had met old men who spoke nostalgically of the Jesuit era, "who
cherished all the customs left by the company, and though they
spoke at secondhand, repeating but the stories they had heard in

youth, kept the illusion that the missions in the Jesuits' time had been a paradise" (x).

Among the political considerations that increased Graham's sympathy for the Jesuits were these: that their paternalistic, feudal-agrarian communities saved the Indians from slavery and commercialism, and that the "half-Arcadian, half-monastic life," with priests working alongside natives, offered some foretaste of a Socialist Utopia. This was "semi-communism" (xii), or at least, being "[a] commonwealth where money was unknown to the majority of the citizens, a sort of dropping down a diving-bell in the flood of progress to keep alive a population which would otherwise soon have been suffocated in its muddy waves" (xiii). When the Jesuits eventually were arbitrarily recalled by decree of King Carlos III in 1767, the settlements fell into ruin, corruption became widespread among the new officials, and the Indians deserted and returned to the woods.

A Vanished Arcadia is centrally, then, not only a vindication of Jesuit rule in Paraguay, drawing on both documents and recollections, but also a sardonic commentary on the myth of progress, the follies of empire, and the erosion of man's achievements by time. The mixture is rich and varied—Graham himself describes it as "a hotch-potch, salmagundi, olla podrida, or sea-pie of sweet and bitter, with perhaps the bitter ruling most" (xiv). Yes, sometimes he is bitter, but the moods vary between the elegiac and the satiric, the sardonic and the earnest. While translating the ancient documents, he likes to draw attention to quirks of phrasing, as when Indians offer the prayer that "the best of birds, the Holy Ghost, may descend upon the King"—"faith grounded, at least, on ornithology," he remarks. The commentary is laced with some of his better cynical epigrams: for example, "Indifference to the feelings of others is perhaps the greatest proof a public man can give of his attachment to the State"; "Historians, like lawyers in conveyancing, catch errors one from another, and transmit them as truths or titles to posterity." And his translations of the documents are frequently enlivened by his recollections, as when he tells of the *alcalde* ("native mayor") at a ruined mission in the 1870s, who used to ride out to greet him, clothed in white, with a cloak of red baize, a large jipijapa hat, and spurs buckled on his naked feet. At the hour of the Angelus, the *alcalde* would kneel to pray wherever the sound might reach him; but all around, the once-cultivated fields had been reconquered by jungle. "On ruined church and chapel, and on broken tower, the lianas climbed as if on trees, creeping up the belfries, and throwing great masses of scarlet and purple flowers out of the apertures where once were hung the bells" (9). There is the tone of an exotic *In Memoriam* about such writing; and he memorializes not only places but forgotten individuals, such as Father Montoya, who led twelve thousand Indians five hundred miles through jungle away from their enemies to sanctuary, like a Moses of the tropics. Graham also brings to life the Indians who, after their communal work, would sometimes garb themselves fantastically for the ceremonial processions in scarlet coats and hats trimmed with gold— a blaze of colors "as gorgeous as a flight of parrots."

Although Cunninghame Graham is keen to praise the Jesuits for having "anticipated Socialism" by their communal organization and their apparent exclusion of the profit motive, he is obliged to note that the priests also introduced such trappings of "a civilized community" as prisons, chains, and whips. He notes drily that bigamy was a crime that the Jesuits chastised severely—"not thinking, being celibates themselves, that not unlikely it was apt to turn into its own punishment without the aid of stripes." Nevertheless, the official decision to abolish the missions by recalling the priests to Spain evokes an eloquently scornful conclusion:

> The self-created goddess Progress was justified by works, and all the land left barren, waiting the time when factories shall pollute its sky, and render miserable the European emigrants, who, flying from their slavery at home, shall have found it waiting for them in their new ꞌaradise beyond the seas. . . . .
>
> Indians and Jesuits are gone from Paraguay, the Indians to that Trapalanda which is their appointed place; and for the Jesuits, they are forgotten, except by those who dive into old chronicles, or who write books, proposing something and concluding nothing, or by travellers, who, wandering in the Tarumensian woods, come on a clump of orange-trees run wild amongst the urundéys. (286, 288)

A prophetic, moving, and memorable conclusion to an utterly distinctive book. Even if the central claim were wrong, the work would still be valuable as creative polemical writing—creative not only because of the descriptive verve but also because of the unusual viewpoint: Jesuits described sympathetically by a skeptic, the Conquest judged by a Socialist, and human nature assessed coolly by a patrician.

The debate about the settlements continues, and *A Vanished Arcadia* is still cited from time to time.[2] Opponents of Graham's view commonly argue that the Jesuits failed to educate the Indians toward independence; they can also claim that the Jesuits helped to bring their expulsion upon themselves by their resistance to early decrees. Some of the Indians entered the settlements not voluntarily but after trickery and capture.[3] There is no doubt, however, that on the whole Graham is correct in his central claim that the Jesuit missions shielded the Indians from the brutal Mamelucos and from enslavement of the kind experienced by the natives of Brazil under the Portuguese. If a choice had to be made, the paternalism of the missions was preferable to the servitude of the plantations. And in any case, few readers now would gainsay his prophetic claim that the European exploitation of Africa would one day be as much execrated as the Spanish conquest of America. When Graham concluded *A Vanished Arcadia* with the words *Finis non coronat opus* ("The end does not crown the work"), he was being too modest; for it could be said that the end provided in the twentieth century by the collapsing prestige of the imperialist ethos has indeed offered the fittest crown for his work.

Subsequent Histories

In the subsequent volumes, Cunninghame Graham's sense of fair play and his scorn for present-day iniquities continued to make him a devil's advocate for the conquistadores, while never losing sight of the plight of the invaded natives.

In stressing that modern imperialists could be quite as ruthless as the Spaniards, Graham was not as original as he claimed. He alleges that the two most celebrated historians of the Conquest, W. H. Prescott and William Robertson, were blinkered by Anglo-Saxon Protestant prejudice; but just as Robertson had conceded that some of the early missionaries had actually championed and defended the natives, so Prescott had advised his readers to note that the Spaniards' atrocities were not a national monopoly but had been emulated subsequently by the British and the French—"Such are the *inevitable* evils of war."[4] The same point was made in Graham's day by a fellow chronicler of the conquistadores, Sir Clements Markham. Graham's *The Conquest of New Granada* (Heinemann, 1922) had been anticipated by a decade by Sir Clements's book of identical title—*The Conquest of New Granada* (Smith, Elder, 1912). A comparison of the two is instructive.

Sir Clements Markham's book is concise, lucid, and rather dry, although written with vigorous moral indignation on behalf of the South American natives. He summarizes the old chronicles, adding little in the way of embellishment. Cunninghame Graham, on the other hand, while largely dependent on exactly the same chronicles (by Fray Simón, Piedrahita, Fray Zamora, etc.), moves through them with much greater freedom, bringing them to life in a variety of ways. He concentrates on personalities, giving fuller treatment to the life of Gonzalo Jiménez de Quesada, the conqueror who played the largest part in establishing Spanish rule in New Granada (which eventually became Colombia). Whereas Markham had curbed speculation, Graham relishes it, speculating freely on Quesada's likely thoughts and feelings during his arduous campaigns. Naturally, Graham uses his recollections of the area to enrich the texture of his account, as in this description of the first Mass of the soldiers on the banks of the Magdalena: "The soldiers knelt on the wet grass, girt with their swords, their lances and their crossbows in their hands. The thin white vapour that envelops everything at that hour on the Magdalena shrouding the forest in its mysterious folds, making the trees look ghostly, and the swirling stream a very Styx or Periphlegethon; the dewdrops falling from the great leaves of unnamed trees, the cries of the nocturnal animals returning from their prowlings to lie hidden in the woods must have made an impression on those fierce and fervent Christians not to be effaced" (42–43).

He retells with verve and enthusiasm the most dramatic incidents of the campaign, as when Quesada and his lieutenant drew their swords and treacherously attempted to capture the King of Tunja, surrounded though he was by crowds of armed Indians. The shouts, the hubbub and confusion, the strange chanciness of Quesada's success—all this, missing from Markham's briefer and dispassionate account, Graham well evokes. And there is certainly no equivalent in Markham's pages for Graham's quirky sense of humor and his eye for odd details in the chronicles. Thus (101): "In the lost 'Memorias' of Quesada, from which Fray Simon occasionally quotes, he says: 'Being upon a journey one day I came to a chief's house, and found him tied to a post with his wives beating him for drunkenness.' " In a footnote Graham has added the dry comment: "This little incident throws a sidelight on polygamy, often lost sight of by monogamists."

Another feature revealed by the comparison is Graham's interest in questioning the methodology of historians by drawing attention to disparities between the chroniclers and to possible discrepancies between what is said to have happened and what is likely to have happened. After citing an eloquent speech attributed to Quesada, Graham typically remarks that this was an admirable address—"if he did make it."

This methodological skepticism had been amply illustrated in the earlier book, *Hernando de Soto,* to which we now turn. In one section, he first cites an incident in Gomara's *History of the Indies:* " 'Soto arrived, making his horse curvet for bravery, or to amaze the Indians, close to the chair on which Atahualpa sat, who did not move although the horse snorted right in his face.' " Then Graham points out that although three chroniclers agree that this was the case, a fourth, the Inca Garcilaso (a name which he spells Garcilasso), treats the tale with scorn, claiming that de Soto was too gentlemanly to let his horse snort in the face of a king. Graham comments: "Weighing the matter up judicially, after the fashion of historians who write at least four hundred years after the facts they touch upon, it seems to-day as if the Inca Garcilasso, in his view of the story, may be justified, as it contains much of that much-bepraised sweet reasonableness to which rude facts so often give the lie" (15–16).

Another of Graham's techniques is to report without comment and with poker-faced solemnity the most unlikely of the incidents: "Just at the hour of twelve . . . . . Satan himself appeared, with a large following of his hellish crew. 'Do not conduct the Spaniards to the land of pearls,' he said. . . . ." (124). Elsewhere he notes with interest that whereas one chronicler says de Soto treated the Indian queen with respect, another alleges that he carried her off by force, while yet another claims that de Soto never met the real queen but only her niece. Graham therefore remarks in a footnote: "I have often thought that a substitute King or Queen, or even a waxwork representation of the real Sovereign, would do quite as well for processions and public ceremonies as the original. The same applies to a President. Indeed, in his case, the thing would be a manifest convenience to himself and all concerned" (128). By such means, Graham succeeds in making a lively, although hardly au-

thoritative, account of Hernando de Soto, who by courage and
ruthlessness won treasure during his Peruvian campaigns, spent it
on his exploration of "La Florida" (during which he discovered the
Mississippi), and finally died of fever in an Indian village whose
very name and site are unknown.

Of the original chronicles of the Conquest, probably the most
interesting and valuable is Bernal Díaz's *Historia verdadera de la
conquista de Nueva España* (circa 1580). Díaz was no learned priest
or scholar but a hardened soldier who had served under Cortés. In
old age, angered by the errors in the chronicles that he had read,
he was moved to write his own account of the campaigns he had
known, and in particular of the long assault by the Spaniards on
the Aztec Empire—the long march from the coast, the entry into
Mexico, with the splendors of Montezuma's court; the strange re-
lationship between Montezuma and Cortés, in which the Aztec's
civilized humanity transcended uncomprehendingly the martial pol-
ity of his destroyer; the pitched battle in which the Mexicans expelled
the invaders from their city; the Spaniards' return, and the siege,
capture, and plundering of Mexico City.

As Díaz was no professional historian, his account is unpolished
and sometimes naive, but still an illuminating eye-witness version:
he has been called the Defoe of chroniclers. To Cunninghame Graham, this roughness of Díaz's narration was a merit: for just as the
paradox-loving Scot had proclaimed "the success of failure" (i.e.,
the superiority of noble endeavor which lacks material reward), so
he from time to time proclaimed that impoverished art might be
superior to opulent art. In the tales "A Repertory Theatre" and
"Los Niños Toreros" he suggests that an amateurish, threadbare
production may be more moving than the affluent one; and he
prefers the rough, manly work of Díaz to a more literary account.
Graham, as a skeptic, particularly liked the episode in which Díaz,
after referring to the historian Gómara's claim that the apostles St.
James and St. Peter actually appeared at one battle, remarked,
"[I]t may be that those of whom Gómara speaks were the glorious
apostles St. Peter and St. James, and I as a sinner was not worthy
to see it. What I saw then and knew was Francisco de Morla on a
bay horse. . . . ." (49). Even in the case of the honest Díaz,
Graham still draws attention to disparities between the words of
the chroniclers and the probable harsh actuality, as here: "Díaz
relates that they took grease from the dead Indians' bodies to cure

their horses with, and says it naturally. He tells us nothing of how the Indians looked cut open with the flies buzzing round their intestines, or says that any of them moved, and that Fulano Sanchez, seeing they still lived, beat out their brains with the butt end of a crossbow. . . . ." (48).

Bernal Díaz del Castillo remains a rather unhappy compromise between Díaz and Graham. If Graham had simply offered his readers a full translation of Díaz's chronicle, that would have been good in principle; or if he had given his own account of the conquest of Mexico, synthesizing the chronicles of Díaz and others, that too would have been good in principle. But what we get is neither. Graham has chosen to offer a résumé—part paraphrase, part quotation, part précis—of much of Díaz's book, interrupting it repeatedly not only with moral reflections but also with assurances that Díaz is a most admirable writer. The effect is of an interesting storyteller being interrupted by a patronizing old chairman.

Díaz has exciting memories to share, when Graham lets him: the memory, for example, of the Spaniards' desperate retreat across the causeway from Mexico City, beset by thousands of Mexicans hurling spears and loosing arrows from the boats that crowded the waterways; or of the time when the Spaniards battling for control of the city saw, on a high platform of the great temple, their captured comrades being ritually sacrificed to the Aztec gods, the victims' palpitating hearts being torn out before the bodies were kicked down the temple steps to be carved into pieces.

As J. M. Cohen has remarked, Graham's book "is most valuable when its author allows Bernal Díaz to speak for himself, but hardly a substitute for his *History.*"[5] The reviews of *Bernal Díaz,* however, as of Graham's histories generally, were on the whole respectfully appreciative. A fair representative is the *Nation*'s review, which said: "Mr. Cunninghame Graham . . . . . is in sympathy with the Spanish character, understands its force and weakness, and judges the deeds (or misdeeds) of the Conquistadores with admirable detachment. He is happy in his subject."[6] Nevertheless, the later volumes in the series (*The Conquest of the River Plate, Pedro de Valdivia,* and *The Horses of the Conquest*) are rather bitty, slipshod and repetitive, and it is not entirely surprising that when D. H. Lawrence reviewed *Pedro de Valdivia* for the *Calendar* the result was a bitter denunciation of the swashbuckling man of action of past and present, whether a Don Pedro or a Don Roberto—the latter being guilty, according to Lawrence, of vanity and complacency.[7] Lawrence complains that Graham fails to indicate the appalling actuality of Valdivia's cruelty to captives. Yet, ironically, Graham could have been Lawrence's mentor in such matters, because (as our example of Díaz and the Indians' grease has shown) the Scot had long been teaching his readers to consider the recalcitrant red actuality behind the gray words of historians. The incident that particularly enraged Lawrence was Valdivia's mutilation of some Araucanian Indians who had opposed his invasion of their lands. The conqueror reported to King Carlos V: "From two hundred of the prisoners I had the hands and noses cut off for their rebellion. . . . ." Graham, however, clearly condemns this act as "cruel barbarism" which failed to intimidate the Indians and stained Valdivia's name indelibly. The cruelty, Graham says, stemmed from the racial prejudice that lives on today. "[Y]our 'poor white trash,' as goes the phrase amongst the negroes in Georgia and in Carolina, cannot endure that a man who has never worn a shoddy suit, and may perhaps be a shade darker than themselves, should dare to equal them" (86).

After battle upon battle against the brave and resourceful Araucanians, Valdivia succeeded in "pacifying" much of Chile and founding a series of townships—Villa Rica, Valdivia, Santiago. The Indians he enslaved, forcing them to work in plantations and mines. Eventually, on an expedition to the besieged fortress of Tucapel, he was ambushed by the natives, and after desperate fighting was captured, stripped, and slaughtered with as much ruthlessness as he had previously shown them. The chronicler Góngora has said: "God has mysteries that a Christian should ponder on. Here was a man feared and obeyed by all, as a great lord, and yet he died a cruel death at the hands of savages." Graham drily echoes his words: "These mysteries are, indeed, well worth a Christian's ponderation . . . . ." (121).

In a long appendix to the book, Graham gives a translation of his main source: the series of reports which Valdivia, in his days as leader and administrator, sent to the Spanish king. It should not be forgotten that by his labors as a translator, Graham made available to English readers important historical documents which previously had been extant only in Spanish.

The next volume, *The Conquest of the River Plate,* deals with the early colonization of much of Argentina and Paraguay, and in particular with the careers of the early governors, including Núñez,

Irala, Centeno, Chávez, Cáceres, and Garay. Some, like Garay (the founder of Buenos Aires) and Chávez, were killed during the incessant battles with the Indians; others, like Cáceres, were overthrown by rivals. Cáceres was actually attacked and seized while attending Mass at a cathedral: supporters of his rival, Bishop Torres, kept him in fetters and sent him back as a prisoner to Spain.

Of all these early governors, the one who, with good reason, commands Graham's greatest interest and admiration is Alvar Núñez. This conquistador was exceptionally humane, by the standards of his day: when Spaniards seized native girls as concubines, he returned the girls to their tribe; when he captured Indians in battle, he soon set them free. He exhorted his soldiers to be slow to enter battle with the natives and, if battle proved unavoidable, to kill as few as possible. Repeatedly he prevented the taking of Indians as slaves.

Probably the main reason for Núñez's exceptional readiness to consider the Indians fellow humans rather than alien objects is that he had lived among them for approximately ten years. Once he had been shipwrecked and captured on the coast by tribesmen; he escaped from this servitude to become a wandering trader among the Indians; and after displaying his skill as a surgeon he acquired a band of faithful followers. When, at the end of those years of wandering, he was at last reunited with fellow Spaniards, "They wished to take some of his followers for slaves, an action Núñez indignantly opposed" (108): with regret, he sent his Indians back into the forest, knowing that they were safer there than among Christians.

Inevitably, as a humane administrator, Núñez annoyed numerous officials, soldiers, and settlers, who regarded slave labor as a natural perquisite of colonization. So he, like Cáceres subsequently, was captured by conspirators and sent to face trial on trumped-up charges; and although absolved, he never returned from Spain to that far-off wilderness in which he had attempted to establish a just and humanitarian policy. It is the life of this brave, far-sighted conquistador which provides the main interest of *The Conquest of the River Plate*.

The last volume in the series, *The Horses of the Conquest,* was certainly both original and logical in conception. The early chronicles frequently noted that the Spanish invaders owed their victories "after God, to the horses." Before the Conquest, the horse was unknown in South America; so when the cavalry disembarked and rode against the Indians, these natives were initially terrified and daunted by the horses, fearing that they might be carnivorous (like the Spaniards' dogs) or even supernatural. Thus, at least in the early stages of the Conquest, the horse was a potent weapon of psychological warfare in addition to providing the conquerors with the customary advantages of speed and mobility. A typical entry, from the chronicles of New Granada, is this: " 'Although the tribes of those valleys put up some resistance, they were soon broken down and routed by the horses (*i.e.* the cavalry), for they held them in such terror that one night, when the Spaniards were encamped close to a little village . . . two or three horses that had got loose, and galloped through the valley neighing and jumping were sufficient to disperse the Indians, who thought they were as ferocious as the bloodhounds, and argued that if dogs made such havoc in their ranks, how much more terrible the larger animal must be' " (22–23).

Graham loved horses. This volume is the one he dedicated to his own favorite, Pampa, whom he had ridden "for twenty years, without a fall." *The Horses of the Conquest* gave him the opportunity to bring together many of the equine incidents and details that he had variously noted in the previous histories. Here again is the account of El Morzillo, the horse of Cortés which, after its death among the Indians, was worshiped by them in effigy as a god (filling the role "as to the manner born"). Here, too, from *Hernando de Soto,* is the tale of Gonçalo Silvestre's epic ride through Florida with his friend Juan Cacho, "the Indians' arrows raining on their armour, like a very hail." And, of course, he recounts Cortés's desperate retreat from Mexico City during the *Noche Triste* when every horse was either killed or wounded. The book, which had begun with a warm tribute to W. H. Hudson, the naturalist, ends with a description of the various types and breeds of horses in South America from the Conquest to the present century.

Looking back over these volumes, we can see that although Cunninghame Graham's series on the Spanish Conquest is, as a whole, rather too selective, quirky, hasty, and polemical to be authoritative, it is too full of documentary source material (often newly translated by Graham) to be a work of popularization. Graham can be an exasperating yet also an endearing guide: he asks intelligent questions about the Conquest and about history in general, even if he does not always provide the answers. Some of his narratives ramble, but when the general itinerary of a campaign has been forgotten, particular incidents rendered by Graham (Alvarado's leap, perhaps, or the death amid fruit of Cortés's horse) remain stark in the memory. And *A Vanished Arcadia* has a good claim to be remembered by posterity, for it amply rewards students not of Paraguay alone, but of human nature.

Cartagena and the Banks of the Sinú

This volume, which appeared in 1920, is a hybrid. The first half is a patchy history of the Colombian area, concentrating on the successive conquistadores and their campaigns, particularly the explorations and battles of Don Pedro de Heredia. The second half describes Cunninghame Graham's journey to and through the region in late 1916 and early 1917, when he surveyed the cattle resources of the area for the British Board of Trade. (The survey had the purpose of improving the wartime supply of beef to Britain, but the shortage of ships stopped the scheme.) The two halves do not link effectively, and the reader may have the feeling (which the later Graham's monographs often engender) that Graham is trying to make a little material go a very long way. The book is at its intermittent best when Graham describes the natural scenery through which he traveled—particularly when he evokes the "miracle" of thousands of bright fish leaping from the river at dawn, when he was canoeing down the San Jorge River at the final stage of his journey. In the course of this patriotic mission, the sixty-four-year-old Graham rode on horseback for ten or eleven hours a day in humid heat, feeling like a battered and broken Don Quixote, he says, before sleeping on some floor with his saddle as a pillow. On the bitterly cold voyage out from England, his ship, the *Cavina,* was in constant danger from submarines and was actually sunk by a torpedo a few months after he disembarked. Although *Cartagena* is one of his weaker books, it still serves as a reminder of the courage and resilience that Cunninghame Graham displayed even in his old age.

Chapter Four

Tales and Essays of His Middle Period

Success

This was a period of prolific writing which produced many of Graham's best tales and sketches. The first collection in this period, *Success*, 1902, is admirably diverse in location and mode. The locations range, if not from China to Peru, at least from the pampas of Argentina to Spain, Scotland, and Pentonville Jail; and the modes vary from philosophical essay to dramatic monologue, from story to descriptive cameo. The melancholy side of Graham's nature and his efforts to be a ruthless realist converge in the high proportion of pieces which end with an image of death, destruction, or decline.

The keynote is sounded in the opening essay, "Success," in which Graham develops his favorite paradox, that failure of worthy endeavor is better than vulgar material success (the alleged "failures" being a remarkably impressive body of famous people—Hannibal, Alcibiades, Raleigh, Mithridates, the Stuarts, Mary Queen of Scots, and even Napoleon); and he links the individual to the national by claiming that Spain, now in decline and defeat, by her cultural heritage still rises above vulgarity.

Tales which emphasize individual death and failure include "Castles in the Air," a melancholy account of an unemployed builder who dies exhausted while seeking work; "Beattock for Moffat," the much-reprinted sketch of a dying Scot making his last journey homeward by rail; and "London," the dismal life-story of a Singhalese girl in the city. A subtler, sensitive version of the theme of defeated or thwarted life is provided by "Postponed," which tells of the Reverend Arthur Bannerman, a widower with two young daughters, who becomes a Roman Catholic priest and consequently suffers bitter pangs of separation from his children. They are consigned to a private school until they may enter a convent, and with difficulty he shuns them for the better service of his God. Graham emphasizes the poignancy of lives blighted emotionally by the religious conscience and by religion itself: in the tradition of Blake and Lawrence he condemns "the mind-forg'd manacles." "How many men before the Rev. Arthur Bannerman have failed to see that there is nothing so materialistic as the mystic and the supernatural . . . . . ?" (118).

The tenor of such tales will remind us of Graham's haughty rebuke to the editor of *Strand Magazine:* "Surely you do not think, from what you may have heard of me, that I would write an optimistic article, if it occurred to me to write a pessimistic article? It is because editors say 'write in this way, or in that,' & writers out of folly or necessity adapt their writings to what is asked for, that there is so much hogwash in English literature" (*LD,* 3). The same endeavor to avoid compromise is evident in the graphic realism with which the sketches "At Utrera" and "Terror" end. In the former, a crowded train pulls out of a Spanish station, leaving a pigeon crushed on the rail; in the latter, amid the traffic of fashionable Belgravia at night, a carriage-wheel runs over a dead cat, "causing its entrails to protrude."

Graham was a Doubting Thomas by nature: he wished to submit all abstract concepts personally to the test of the senses. A favorite device of his, therefore, was to resolve a discussion or a survey with a close-up of some somber, bloody, or unsavory detail. This technique was certainly encouraged by Edward Garnett, who in his letters repeatedly warned Graham of the dangers of diffuseness and of the value of the unexpected image which focuses and coordinates the sketch. Earlier we saw how, with characteristic intelligence and urgency, he had commended the recurrent bird-cage image in the tale "S.S. *Atlas*" ("those cages are a centre, a symbol amid the welter & jumble"), and he added: "I sue for the artist in you, the artist you concealed so long under the man of action, the artist that is the most important now."[1]

Related to the technique of the final focus on some unexpected detail is the technique of "life observed from the wings"—the use of oblique scrutiny, with the action seen sidelong rather than from the stalls. Graham, a keen student of the visual arts and their modern developments, could have seen many instances of the oblique viewpoint in Impressionist canvases, particularly those of Degas and

Manet. In *Success,* the tale "The Pyramid" uses this technique quite overtly and literally: Graham, observing the performers at a music-hall as though he were at the side of the stage, is able to note the glare of hatred and contempt that a young acrobat, precariously balanced at the pinnacle of a human pyramid, directs at the applauding spectators.

"Might, Majesty, and Dominion" is another effective example of this inherently ironic and probing technique. In this case it is fused with the device of final focus on some base detail. The piece describes the public mourning for Queen Victoria, and at the outset the irony is imperceptible: "A nation dressed in black, a city wreathed in purple hangings, woe upon every face, and grief in every heart. . . . . Not only for the passing of the Queen, the virtuous woman, the good mother, the slave of duty; but because she was the mother of her people, even the poorest of her people in the land." Then Graham surveys the achievements of her reign: the national wealth increased, the empire extended, battleships built, and a new era created by steam and electricity. He surveys, too, the procession of mourners: emperors and kings, "the martial pomp and majesty of glorious war clattering and clanking at their heels." Eventually, the crowds disperse, leaving a scum of wind-blown sandwich-papers which two dogs sniff at. Then:

Lastly, a man grown old in the long reign of the much-mourned ruler, whose funeral procession had just passed, stumbled about, slipping upon the muddy grass, and taking up a paper from the mud fed ravenously on that which the two dogs had looked at with disdain.

His hunger satisfied, he took up of the fragments that remained a pocketful, and then, whistling a snatch from a forgotten opera, slouched slowly onward and was swallowed by the gloom. (85)

These last two pieces are among the best in the book, although varied pleasures are also offered by "Los Seguidores," "Un Infeliz," and the autobiographical account of Pentonville Jail, "Sursum Corda."

"Los Seguidores" begins by describing two horses which are as brothers, so closely do they stay together; then we learn of their owner, Cruz Cabrera, and of the largely unconscious sexual rivalry which slowly develops between Cruz and his brother Froilán, a rivalry for their half-sister. The tale's climax is a sudden incursion of violence as Froilán dies on his own knife; and finally the two horses bear the living and the dead rivals to the cemetery. An ironic disparity between the "brotherhood" of men and the saner brotherhood of animals is quietly and effectively implied. The subsequent piece, "Un Infeliz," describes a chance encounter with an engineer in Algeria. This stoical, shabby widower reviews his impoverished life as the carriage rattles on to his destination, a desolate settlement by a mine-working. Both the character and the setting, and the sad appropriateness of each for the other, are well evoked.

By contrast, "Sursum Corda" [Lift Up Your Hearts] takes us to Pentonville Prison and Graham's sojourn there in 1888. He recalls the tedium of the solitary cell and the oakum-picking, but also the great communal release of noise and energy permitted by the hymn-singing on Sundays: "the chapel quivers like a ship from stem to stern, dust flies, and loud from every throat the pious doggerel peals. And in the sounds the prison melts away. . . . ." (97). This piece contains a passing tribute to Oscar Wilde's recent writings on imprisonment; and we may be reminded by it that when Wilde was disgraced and generally shunned after being sentenced for homosexuality, Graham sent him consolatory letters praising "The Ballad of Reading Gaol." Just as Graham had gone out of his way to shake hands in Parliament with the disgraced Parnell, so now he sympathized with the fallen Wilde. From Paris, where he was using the name "Sebastian Melmoth," the playwright replied: "I . . . . . wish we could meet to talk over the many prisons of life—prisons of stone, prisons of passion, prisons of intellect, prisons of morality, and the rest—all limitations, external or internal, are prison-walls—and life is a limitation" (*WD,* 307).[2]

Progress

Progress (1905) is less satisfactory a volume than *Success,* having rather too many slight and diffuse pieces. Graham's techniques are sometimes reminiscent of those of a boy in a slow bicycle game—seeing how slowly he can make the bicycle go without actually falling off. Or, to use Laurence Davies's more complimentary analogy: "the method is almost like that of the legendary gourmet who cooked an anchovy inside a lark, the lark inside a quail, the quail inside a chicken, the chicken inside an ox, threw away the accompaniments and ate the anchovy" (*LD,* 137). In "McKechnie *v.*

Scaramanga," McKechnie admits that his tale rambles—"I'm sort o' wandered. . . . . I'm subject to thae digressions; so was Sir Walter Scott and others I could mention" (207–8), but the admission does not constitute atonement. The collection is in the main a gallery of character studies of various people encountered by Graham in Entre Ríos, San Antonio, Morocco, and other far-off localities; but "A Yorkshire Tragedy" describes the aftermath of the Featherstone Pit killings of 1893, while "Snow in Menteith," "The Laroch," "Pollybaglan," and "A Traveller" are richly descriptive of the Scottish countryside that Graham had come to know intimately during his early years at Gartmore.

The subtlest piece is probably the last, "A Vestal," which tells how the mistress of a Spanish gentleman, living with him at a continental hotel, first shocks the conventional, then is gradually accepted, and, as she outlives the man, becomes an institution— a touching, pathetic, slightly ludicrous figure surviving in draftily ornate discomfort, her sole companion a gray parrot which whistles sea-chanties and curses in English. By such incongruous detail Graham wins belief from the reader and resists the undertow of the sentimental—always a danger to a writer who so often adopts a melancholy or elegiac tone.

Although *Progress* is a relatively mild volume, the *Spectator* found it shocking, claiming that its "lapses in taste" and "violent and even disgusting phrases" were sufficient to "render it unsuitable for general perusal" (11 February 1905, 221). (Graham retorted that the magazine was "a spinster-like old harlot.") The critic may have been offended, among other details, by the passing description— very reticent by today's standards—of rape and carnage in the tale "His Return," in which Bu'Horma loves and loses a tall Arab girl who has been allotted to him "reeking . . . . . from the hot kisses of her ravishers" (157).

His People

Cunninghame Graham was always provoked rather than deterred by censorious critics, and the next volume, *His People,* 1906, includes "Signalled," a sympathetic sketch of a fleeting friendship between a prostitute and an uncomprehending English girl; while in "Le Chef " and "Gualeguaychú," his reminiscences of the early days in Argentina include the customary frank notation of the kinds and classes of prostitutes (70–71, 142–43, 147) down to the lowest extreme—among the huts in a lane where half-caste and foreign girls, too coarse for the city, sat painted at their doors.

> Vice was so unattractive, set as it was in a mud hovel, thatched with straw, that many, whom the love of virtue bound but lightly, yet were virtuous from disgust. Whether the moral gain was great, only the moralist can say, and he was an infrequent visitor in those days, either at Ellerman's or at the Fonda del Vapór. In fact morality was looked at in the larger or the Latin way, with the result that on the whole life was far cleaner than in Anglo-Saxon lands, where nature being what it is, the same things happen but are rendered meaner by concealment; the homage, as they say, vice pays to virtue, but which makes virtue, as it were, compound a felony and smirches both of them. ("Gualeguaychú," 143)

Graham was also criticized, and with reason, for haste and casualness of writing; but some of the pieces in this and the previous volume ("The Laroch," "Snow in Menteith," "Tobar na Reil," "The Grey Kirk," and "Fate") tend toward a contrasting fault. These pieces are self-consciously stylish and "literary," fancifully romantic and melancholy; they have that deliberate eloquence which once would have gratified an anthologist, but which can generate clichés of phrase and feeling that are made the more conspicuous by our present iron age of resistance to the lyrical. The ending of "Fate" illustrates both the eloquence and those dangers to which the archaism and stock phrase ("tarry longer" and "scant comprehension") are the indices. "My fellow-sufferer by fate"—thus the narrator addresses a moth that died, trapped behind the glass of a picture-frame—"you, who left instantly the world in which we tarry longer instants, with as scant comprehension of our lives perhaps as you, do not forget us prisoned in our glass; but in the limbo where you flutter now, think that a fellow-moth remembers you, just as you lived and died, with your soft body, iridescent wings, and sharp antennae" (*His People,* 200).

Yet, in complete contrast, the same collection also offers one of the most vigorously incisive of his biographic articles, "A Memory of Parnell," which well conveys the power, authority, and ruthless fanaticism of the Irish Nationalist leader in Parliament. "He would remark half confidentially to his lieutenant, 'Biggar, I think that this debate ought not to finish before twelve o'clock.' To which his Sancho Panza would reply, 'It's quite impossible; I've let the boys away.' Then, absently, as if he had never seen the man, or at that instant suddenly became aware that he persisted still in living, Parnell would say, 'Tell Gallagher to speak.' 'Gallagher, sir, the only thing he knows is butter.' 'Well, let him speak on butter.' " For an hour or more, with sweat running down his face, Gallagher would tell the House that the bill under discussion would be unjust to Ireland in general and her butter in particular. Then—"Just about midnight Parnell might saunter in and either say 'I think I will not speak,' or 'Biggar, tell that fool to stop; I wish to say a word.' Then word would somehow be conveyed to the rapt orator, who would subside, perhaps in the very middle of a phrase, and Parnell, rising, would proceed, apparently quite coldly, but with shut fists, and a light foam about the corners of his mouth, to distil vitriol, drop by drop, into the very souls of Englishmen, till Gladstone, putting on his hat, would leave the House. . . . . ." (283–84). Parnell's career was wrecked by the scandal which resulted from his adultery with the wife of a supporter; but, to Graham, he remained a great man in a world of mediocrities: "the multitude of rats has been the undoing of the lion" (275).

"Le Chef," with its recollections of Buenos Aires in the 1870s and 1880s, offers rich material both for the would-be biographer of Graham and for the historian of bygone life in South America. With customary sharp clarity of recall he looks back over thirty years at the various emigrants (known as "The Gentle Shepherds") who gathered at Claraz's Hotel on the corner of the Calle de Cangallo: there was bearded Long John Arbuthnott, who was eventually lost at sea while sailing in a schooner to the Falkland Isles, Lucien Simmonet, a young Parisian journalist who earned his living "by writing paragraphs from Paris in a back street in Buenos Aires," and Dunsmere—each in his turn illumined by a rapid hovering of Graham's memory over some concrete detail associated with that person. Thus: "Dunsmere was lost in those vague regions known as 'down about the Straits'; all that remains of him is a blue poncho barred with red, which lay for years upon his father's sofa in his smoking-room, and a whip made of coronilla wood mounted with silver, which when I used to take it up from where it lay, would bring him back to me, and make the tears stand in his father's eyes, who knew instinctively where and with whom my thoughts were straying, whilst I held it in my hand" (74–75). Much as Graham admired tougher literary models, something of the eighteenth century's "Cult of Sensibility" and even of Henry Mackenzie's *The Man of Feeling* from time to time softens his work.

The same piece contains some sharp notation of the impact of "progress" on Buenos Aires even in the two years between Graham's first arrival in 1870 and his return later. No longer did whaleboats carry the travelers the ten or twelve miles to the shore from the ships out there on the thick yellow water of the River Plate; "nor did a cart drawn by three horses with a Basque riding the near-side animal, or a bullock-wagon with a man seated on the yoke, carry one to the shore where the water shoaling made it unsafe for boats." Instead, steam launches rushed through the choppy waves to the metal pier which had now replaced the ancient wooden wharf. And in the city, the house of the conquistador Garay had been demolished.

The narration finally concentrates on Louis Cossart, the chef of the title, who with his mistress Emilienne runs a dusty, fly-blown restaurant and dreams of making his fortune in London. Many years later, while riding his horse to Hyde Park past St. Peter's in Eaton Square, Graham sees Cossart emerging from the church in a frock-coat with a gardenia in his buttonhole. "His hat shone shiny as a life-guardsman's helmet, and was cocked at such an angle on his head, it seemed capillary attraction only could keep it in its place. His boots were like the top layer of a pot of jelly, and in his hand he had a silver-mounted cane, the crutch of which was ivory, shaped like a woman's leg. In his left hand he held new gloves of a bright *sang de boeuf,* and on his cheek the barber's powder clung, like sugar on a cake" (92–93). He is now the chef of a London club, and has succeeded in his ambition; but what his meeting with Graham emphasizes is the distance traveled by both men, in time, space, and experience, from those early hopeful and irresponsible years at Claraz's Hotel in bygone Argentina.

Another of the longer pieces in this collection is "Miss Christian Jean," which has a Scottish setting. Laurence Davies says "[Graham] is interested, it is true, in the value of shared memory as social bond and comfort, but 'Miss Christian Jean' . . . . . , which studies this function, also reveals memory's unpredictability." Whereas a more professional or orthodox writer would manipulate the material, "Graham lets his own and his characters' recollection play free, and the result is less sentimental, more disquieting" (*LD,* 174). Graham's essay begins with characteristic obliqueness: he recalls his earliest days at Gartmore, the ancestral home with its smell of damp and kingwood furniture and roses dried in bowls. He remembers in particular two third-rate landscape paintings which to him were more interesting, because of their clumsy oddity, than the master-pieces by Reynolds and Raeburn which hung on the walls. "It may be, too, that the unnatural landscape [in the paintings] caused me to form unnatural views of life, finding things interesting and people worthy of remark whom others found quite commonplace, merely upon their own account, and not from the surroundings of their lives" (217). This is a crucial statement. It is true to Graham's obsessive need to memorialize human life anywhere, without the artificial imposition of further significance; *to value it merely and sufficiently because it is life.*

Gradually the narrative introduces Laird Wallace, Wallace of Gartchorrachan, a neighbor who tells of the death of his old aunt. Death had come to Miss Christian Jean in the depths of winter when the whole region was beset by snow and ice. "At last I reached the avenue, the mare fair taigled [wearied], and the ice hanging from her fetlocks and her mane and wagging to and fro. The evergreens were, so to speak, a-wash, and looked like beds of parsley or of greens, and underneath the trees the squirrels' footsteps in the snow seemed those of some strange birds, where they had melted and then frozen on the ground. Across the sky a crow or two flew slowly, flapping their wings as if the joint oil had been frozen in their bones and cawing sullenly" (231). The coffin is delayed by the snows, but eventually it arrives, and Wallace and the old butler have to lower Aunt Christian into it.

"A week had passed and she looked black and shrunken, and as I lifted her, the chill from the cold flesh struck me with horror, and welled into the bones. I could not kiss her as she lay like a mummy in the kist [coffin], for the shrunk face with the white clothes about the chin was not the same Aunt Christian's, who I had loved and before whom I had trembled for so many years, but changed somehow and horrible to see.
 . . . . . What the old butler did, I do not mind; but I just dandered out into the garden, and washed my hands in snow. . . . . ." (234)

This is a gently flowing, ruminative piece, and doubtless Graham wrote it as naturally as it occurred to him; but at some, possibly unconscious, level his imagination seems to have been coordinating various parts of it. The narrative's final emphasis on the chilling and horrible transformation wrought by death serves to justify the very habit of mind that Graham had proclaimed as his own in the earlier pages: that habit of valuing life "on its own account."

Faith, Hope, and *Charity*

In the subsequent series of volumes, *Faith, Hope,* and *Charity,* Cunninghame Graham continues his defiance of convention and propriety with several tales about prostitutes, brothels, and the "kept woman." This group includes "Dutch Smith," "Un Monsieur," "Buta," the Preface to *Charity,* "Un Autre Monsieur," and "Christie Christison"; "La Alcaldesa" relates to it. "Pimps and prostitutes are everywhere," said an infuriated and uncharitable reviewer of *Charity.* "Even on his damned pampas incest is only avoided by murder. So all his 'literary distinction,' his 'quaint ironical philosophy,' his 'pleasing whimsicality,' is to be sought in the fact that he tells smoke-room stories to a mixed audience" (*New Age,* 21 March 1912, 496).

The smoke-room story instrumentalizes the whore; Graham does the opposite: he humanizes her. Generally he looks with warm sympathy on the prostitute, whether she be the girl who pitiably succumbs to circumstances, like the Rahma of "Buta" (the title means "Whore"), or the intelligent and sophisticated Elise of "Un Monsieur" and "Un Autre Monsieur" (the real "Elise" being well known to Graham). The most subtle of such tales is "Christie Christison," which, by means of two apparently random yet thematically interlinked incidents, makes the point that the Indian who attempts to buy Christie's wife for himself (with fifty dollars, a horse, and some skins) is morally no worse, and certainly less hypocritical, than the Christians who profess to be civilized and yet on Sunday at a brothel buy for cash the sexual services of a married woman. What Graham criticizes is not prostitution but the arrogant hypocrisy— not only of a civilization which both condemns and maintains the brothel but also of the male sex which regards the whore as immoral yet her client as properly virile.

There was a symbolic inevitability about Graham's sympathy with the prostitute. He felt that in his deeds as a traveler and man of action he was expressing the manly side of his nature, while in his work as a writer he was expressing a feminine and even self-prostituting side. One connection was this: a prostitute offers her intimate self to the public, at a price; and Graham, in his strongly autobiographical work, was offering his intimate self (his memory and emotions) to the public, at a price—the price of the books. When his literary friends Conrad and Garnett wrote to him not to comment on his works but to offer commiserations over the sale of Gartmore, he said of their concern: "It I think affects me, as if a man were to kiss a whore on the mouth & to say he loved her, apart from whoredom."[3] And in a subsequent preface, he made the strangely revealing claim: "Men write against their will, constrained by some fell power, that they know perfectly they should resist, but cannot for their life; just as they say that sometimes women suffering violence have seized their violators round the neck and kissed them fiercely, as though not knowing what they did, or yielding to temptation, just as a writer does. . . . ."[4]

Technically, "Christie Christison" illustrates Cunninghame Graham's increasing proficiency in oblique narrative—the use of the tale within a tale, or the reminiscences of a distinctive character: a device which, by curbing Graham's personal expatiations, sometimes increases the depth of implication: reticence generates resonance. In this oblique narrative technique, Graham may have been encouraged by the tales of his friend Conrad, particularly those in which Marlow figures ("Youth," *Heart of Darkness,* and *Lord Jim*), although it was naturally a widely used technique at this period—Maupassant, Turgenev, Kipling, James, and Wells were proficient in it. "Christie Christison" certainly shows that Graham soon became adept at exploiting the disparity between the viewpoint of the fictional narrator and that of his hearers: the dour Scottish character with his tang of dialect proves to have had a richer and more bizarre life than the cosmopolitan listeners had suspected. The mundane features conceal a tough wisdom.

Cunninghame Graham had shown that he was prepared to defend the rights of women and even of prostitutes; and in the tale "Mirahuano" *(Hope)* he speaks on behalf of blacks. Racial prejudice was so endemic in his times, among all classes, that in his work (as in the work of Conrad) what we see is not an immediate or automatic opposition to racial prejudice but something more complicated. There is a measure of endorsement of that prejudice when the writer's imagination and judgment are only partly engaged, followed by a growing liberation from, and scorn for, that prejudice as they become more fully engaged. Elsewhere, in conversation, in casual references in letters, or in lesser published work, he may echo the racialism of his times; but in a careful tale like "Mirahuano," the humanity speaks clearly and firmly.

This piece tells of a black poet who is patronized by the citizens of a South American republic "in which by theory all men were free and equal by the law." His white friends wish him *buenos noches* as they enter their houses, to which he is never invited except on business. After years of such measured toleration comes the moment of his outburst. "Think of my life; my very God is white, made in your image, imposed upon my race by yours. His menacing pale face has haunted me from childhood, hard and unsympathetic, and looking just as if He scorned us whom you call His children, although we know it is untrue. Your laws are all a lie. His too, unless it is that you have falsified them in your own interests and to keep us slaves" (117). Eventually, a countryman finds the poet's body in a backwater: he pulls it out, removes and dries the clothes for sale, and pushes the corpse back into the stream. The tale thus suggests that mere toleration without human concern may in the long term be sometimes as lethal as more aggressive forms of prejudice.

A Hatchment and *Brought Forward*

A Hatchment (1913) maintains the standards of proficiency (within his slight and minor genres) attained by Graham in *Hope* and *Charity*. This volume includes further detailed recollections of the early days in Argentina and Uruguay: "Los Indios," "A Retrospect," "The Pass of the River," "Anastasio Lucena," and particularly "El Rodeo," with its graphic account of the gauchos' skills and their perils in stampedes. He sentimentalizes neither the gauchos nor their work, noting the routine of washing maggots out of cows' sores with salt and water, or the ruthlessness with which the men curbed a bullock with a tendency to escape by dissecting a length of skin between the eyes so that it fell and blinded the animal. If meat were needed, and the chosen bull relatively tame, the gaucho would, after lassoing it, directly cut its throat: "The gushing stream of blood sprang like the water from a fire-plug, and the doomed creature sank upon its knees, then rocked a little to and fro, and with a bellow of distress, fell and expired" (63). If, on the other hand, the animal were fierce, the gaucho would after its capture slash its hocks to hamstring it;

the bullock would jump about in agony upon its mutilated legs; and not till it was rendered quite helpless would the man approach to administer the death-blow.

"The Pass of the River" recalls the days when at a pulpería it was quite customary for a pair of gauchos to challenge each other to a friendly knife-fight to pass the time. Blows to the body were prohibited, and sometimes only an inch or so of blade was exposed. "Usually, after springing to and fro like cats, parrying, passing and crouching low, catching the blows upon their arms defended by their summer *ponchos,* they would pause for breath, whilst the assistants criticized the strokes. As all the cuts were levelled either at the arm or face, the contest sometimes lasted five or six minutes, and when at last the blood was drawn the beaten man, calling for wine, handed it courteously to his opponent, who passed it back to him, with many compliments" (121–22). By contrast, "Anastasio Lucena" is a tale, ostensibly told by George Morton Mansel, of a blind and gentle gaucho who had once shown him hospitality on a journey. Mansel's prefatory remarks are appropriate to much of Graham's work. "After expelling through his mouth and nostrils a sort of solfatara of blue smoke, he said: 'Yes, call my yarn a memory, a recollection . . . for it is not a story, only a circumstance that I remember vividly, just as one never can forget an object seen in a flash of lightning . . . perhaps the word should be . . .' One of us interjected 'An Impression'; he nodded. . . . ." (132–33). And indeed the tale does finally preserve a sharp impression of the tall gaucho with his long black hair just flecked with gray: "His head was turned towards the sound of the black-cream-colour's hoofs, and his eyes, open but sightless, seemed to take in the Pampa with its indomitable space" (142–43).

In this collection, "Bismillah" is a Moroccan description, an Arcadia which typically contains its death, here the sudden slaughter of a kid. Scottish reminiscences continue with "Mist in Menteith," "Falkirk Tryst," and "Loose and Broken Men." "A Page of Pliny" tells of Graham's ill-fated gold-prospecting expedition in Spain, while "A Belly-God" offers a wry anecdote ostensibly told by "the Minister of Costalarga," in real life Don Santiago Pérez Triana of Colombia, who had earlier contributed to Conrad's *Nostromo.* (In that novel, Pérez Triana's ideas are bestowed on Don José Avellanos, statesman of Costaguana, while his plump physique is lent to Don Vincente Ribiera, the rotund, bespectacled president-dictator.) This is a subtly modulated tale which blends the sad, the ludicrous, the touching, and the absurd. It well establishes and contrasts the characters of the minister, the shy and penurious Englishman whom he employs as a secretary, and the envious porter. As the narrative concerns the tragicomic effects of a failure of communication between the secretary and his employer, the descriptive coda makes an effectively ironic thematic comment. For there, outside the minister's window, a soldier is "in animated conversation" with a girl he has accosted; nearby is a fountain with the statue of a nymph holding a conch-shell. "The nymph, standing dejectedly upon her dolphin in the water-basin, was the sole witness of their interview. The conch-shell, seen from the side on which they sat, looked a little like an ear-trumpet which she had turned to spy upon their talk and catch their confidences. They did not heed it. . . . ." (211). This is one of Graham's best-managed anecdotes.

The gallery of family portraits is extended in "A Moral Victory," the tale of a concupiscent uncle whose wife adroitly takes the place in his cabin that he had arranged for a seafaring mistress. "A Hatchment" offers a gentle ruminative obituary for George Morton Mansel, the ex-seaman who (as "Anastasio Lucena" had reminded us) had once gone riding, drinking and horse-trading with Graham through Uruguay and Brazil, but who, forty years later, had become a solitary reclusive figure reading and dozing before the fire in his decaying manor-house near Dorchester. (Thomas Hardy, who lived on the outskirts of Dorchester, knew Mansel and corresponded with Graham. He would have appreciated both the stoical melancholy of these sketches and Graham's disdain for man's inhumanity to man.)

Brought Forward (1916), a less substantial volume, concludes this middle period; indeed, according to the deftly oblique preface, it concludes Graham's whole career as a writer, for he assures the reader that he is now putting the pen down finally before death or public scorn overtakes him. This assurance, and the tone of the preface, were of course belied by subsequent volumes; no doubt the perils of wartime had occasioned Graham's sense of imminent termination. The war variously overshadows this collection: "Brought Forward" is a patriotic tale of a Clydeside worker who enters the army to avenge a fallen friend; "Elysium" looks sympathetically at a soldier home on leave; "Uno dei Mille" approves Italian emigrants in South America who are returning to Europe to fight the Germans; and

"In a Backwater" offers a bucolic judgment of the wastefulness of war.

The most personal and poignant essays in the volume are "Los Pingos" and "Bopicuá," in which Graham recalls his recent experiences in Uruguay, where he, although a lifelong defender of animals and lover of horses, found himself led by patriotism to round up the steeds needed by the British army in Europe. "Slowly Arena, El Correntino, Paralelo, Suarez, and the rest drove the herd to pasture in the deep lush grass. The rest of us rode up some rising ground towards the wood. There we drew up, and looking back towards the plain on which the horses seemed to have dwindled to the size of sheep in the half-light, some one, I think it was Arena, or perhaps Pablo Suarez, spoke their elegy: 'Eat well,' he said; 'there is no grass like that . . . . . where you go across the sea. The grass in Europe all must smell of blood' " (205).

In contrast to these thoughtful pieces is the unfortunate "El Tango Argentino," in which Graham subjects the fashionable life of an opulent Parisian hotel to a rather crude and facile satiric scorn, here clearly tainted by anti-Semitism. "Lesbos had sent its legions;" Americans boast about their wealth; and "Jews and more Jews, and Jewesses and still more Jewesses, were there, some of them married to Christians and turned Catholic, but betrayed by their Semitic type, although they talked of Lourdes and of the Holy Father with the best" (83). The demonstration of the tango at the hotel is regarded by Graham with puritanical contempt ("the dancers' efforts at indecency had been appreciated"), and he seeks imaginative refuge in the Argentina of the past, where the tango was danced with stately gravity. That the dance he recalls is interrupted by a melodramatic knife-fight in which one gaucho murders another may lead the reader to distrust Graham's intended contrast between urban decadence and pastoral health.

Another tale in this collection, "Feast Day in Santa Maria Mayor," brings before us, once again, Enrique Clerici, the bartender of Itapuá. This reappearance draws attention to an extensive critical matter which we may term that of *transtextualities*.

Transtextualities

A transtextuality occurs when a particular character appears in two or more separate works. The reader who is familiar with a previous appearance by that character will take a different view of him from that of a reader who knows only the later instance. The probability (although not a certainty) is that the former reader will have a stronger sense of the character's authenticity—he'll be an old acquaintance. If we look, for example, at works by Graham's friend, Conrad, we find that in *The Shadow-Line* we meet an obnoxious fellow called Hamilton who is failing to pay his debts at a Sailors' Home. Many years previously Conrad had published the tale "The End of the Tether," in which the narrator had referred to a fellow called Hamilton who had failed to pay his debts but who was at last sent away to a ship at Saigon. The reader who knows "The End of the Tether" will, when he comes to *The Shadow-Line,* regard Hamilton not only as a familiar character but will also see his activities in an ironic light, for he already knows about his undignified departure. One narrative thus sustains the other. And transtextuality can occur on a very large scale. Thus what may be termed "The Biography of Tom Lingard" is sustained through three Conradian novels *(Almayer's Folly, An Outcast of the Islands,* and *The Rescue)* which trace his life in reverse order from his old age to his prime; while "The Biography of Charles Marlow" is a narrative that we may reconstitute from the various works in which Marlow appears (*"Youth," Heart of Darkness, Lord Jim, Chance*). That Marlow remains unmarried in *Chance* charges with retrospective poignancy his failure of communication with the girl in *Heart of Darkness* whose portrait had brought a stirring of love to him.

Numerous tales by Cunninghame Graham are interlaced by transtextualities. Elise appears in "Un Monsieur" and "Un Autre Monsieur," Mansel in "The Ipané" (as "Hansel"), "A Hatchment," "Anastasio Lucena " and elsewhere, Clerici in "Cruz Alta," "The Captive," "Feast Day in Santa Maria Mayor," and "The Stationmaster's Horse"; while other recurrent figures are Cossart, Claraz, Bibi Carleton, and Dr. Stewart, and gauchos like Paralelo, Suárez, and Pájaro (alias Páncharo). They recur because, most obviously, they had real existence and came to Graham's mind naturally on different occasions; but the effects of the recurrences are various. One is to increase our confidence in the authenticity of the recollections. Another is incremental: the characters gain in substance at each appearance because we carry over in memory some of the descriptive matter of their previous manifestation. There may also be an increase in emotional resonance: for example, we are the more concerned that Elise in "Un Autre Monsieur" will regain her health and perhaps enter a contented marriage, because of our memory of the unjust way in which she was treated in "Un Monsieur." Another example: the account of the aged Mansel's decline and death in "A Hatchment" will be the more poignant for those who have met the younger, adventurous Mansel in "The Ipané" or in the tale which, with perhaps accidental irony, appeared in the same volume as "A Hatchment," "Anastasio Lucena." Such effects may encourage us to explore more extensively the range of Graham's works. Perhaps the most interesting effect of all comes when we discover that transtextuality occurs not only *within* Graham's *œuvre* but also *between* his and another writer's: as when we see that the real Enrique Clerici of Paraguay, after journeying through Graham's pages, is eventually translated into Giorgio Viola of Costaguana in Conrad's *Nostromo*. Here we not only see but participate in a transtextual translation from historic actuality into literary immortality.

Chapter Five
The Biographies

It will already be clear that, in religious matters, Cunninghame Graham's attitudes were variable. In his more cynical and Voltairian moods, he could mock virtually all forms of religion as "a wall of cobwebs," the absurd construction of vain and fallible mortals. Sometimes he was antitheistic, for (like Algernon Swinburne, Thomas Hardy, and, later, Albert Camus) he was capable of imagining God as real but hostile, a remote and callous deity to be defied. At other times, he was the shoulder-shrugging agnostic, tolerant and noncommittal (who knows what lies beyond?), or even the wistful dreamer about some pampa or Trapalanda in the sky. Occasionally, as in "The Fourth Magus" or "Upwards," he appears to be moved by the Christian faith and almost to regret the central lack of belief that holds him back, so that he resembles the Italian peasant in the latter tale who looks on the crib but can see only the animals and not the Christ. The Augustan, skeptical, empirical side of his nature, inherited largely from his mother, encourages Graham to look with a satirical eye or a world-weary head-shake on religious fanatics and mystics; yet his Romantic spirit and his scorn for bourgeois materialism and its prudential compromises encourages him (the son of a loving but deranged father) to see such fanatics in a charitable and sometimes almost admiring way, too. Such religious extremists of West and East had already been the subject of short pieces, "Father Archangel," "El Jehad," "Progress," and "A Sebastianist"; and in *A Brazilian Mystic* (1920) he devoted a whole book to one.

President Roosevelt had urged him to write about Brazil, and when wartime service brought Graham to Bahía on the Brazilian coast, Don José María Braceras suggested the subject.[1] The mystic in question is Antonio Maciel (circa 1835–1897), a quiet storekeeper whose character was transformed when his wife eloped with a police officer. Maciel attacked one of her relatives, was jailed, escaped, and became a wanderer in the wilderness. "The smug cashier, dressed carefully in white drill and clean straw hat, had vanished, and in his place Antonio Maciel appeared—an anchorite. Sunburned and worn with fasting, his eyes wide open, fixed and staring, his sunken face, and his thin limbs, worn with privation, gave him the look of a monk from the Thebais. . . . . He was not mad, and yet not altogether sane, but probably just on that borderland in which dwell saints and visionaries, and all those folk who feel they have a mission to declare, a world to save, and a vague Deity they have to glorify" (68).

Maciel's reputation as a seer grew; miracles were attributed to him; and gradually he attracted a large and motley band of followers—the halt and lame, the simple and superstitious, the criminal and fanatical. He established a "holy city" at Canudos in the heart of the Sertão, the remote and rugged backlands of Brazil, where his followers (the Jagunços) prayed, sang, drank, fornicated, and awaited the coming of Antichrist and then of the Redeemer, "that Don Sebastian who . . . . . should come to rule the world in glory, blot out injustice, cast down the mighty, and exalt the poor in spirit, giving them the world as their inheritance" (237–38).

If Antichrist arrived, however, it was evidently in the form of the Brazilian government, which sent wave after wave of military expeditions against the citadel of Maciel the Counselor (el Conselheiro). And if the army had the equipment—the Krupp machine guns, the rifles and bayonets—Maciel and his followers had cunning, knowledge of the terrain, and the selfless courage of fanaticism. Repeatedly the troops were ambushed, outwitted, and mauled during the sieges. The very streets of Canudos proved a death-trap in which shots were fired point-blank through crevices in the walls while hot water, stones, and burning tarred rope were hurled down on the soldiers' heads; and the background music, beyond the shrieks of the wounded and the roar of explosions, was the psalmody and triumphant hymn-singing of El Conselheiro's followers. The dead soldiers were decapitated, their heads impaled on stakes on each side of the defile between Canudos and Mount Cambaio. Above each head, on the trees and bushes, hung remnants of uniform and equipment—a belt, jacket, or cloak, "so that the whole road seemed a rag-fair, of death" (195).

Lastly, impaled and standing upright, shrivelled to a mummy in the dry air of Sertão, they stuck the body of Colonel Tamarindo, as if he still commanded his unlucky men, placing it only a yard or two from where he fell. His horse, mortally wounded, had staggered a few paces farther on before it died upon its feet, resting against a bank. The Jagunços left it where it had finished its career, and the dry climate desiccated it, so that months afterwards, when a new expedition passed through the defile, it was still perfect, undecayed and dry, with the wind lifting up its mane occasionally—a veritable pale horse of death, descended lineally from its prototype in the Apocalypse. (195)

Inevitably, law, order, and civilization, represented by yet greater concentrations of even more heavily armed troops, took their vengeance; and after massive bombardments and protracted sieges it was the lot of the starving Jagunços finally to be slaughtered in ones and twos, while the Counselor himself died in his ruined church, clasping a silver crucifix to his breast. "His face was calm, his body almost mere skin and bones, worn out with fasting and with the death of his illusions, but his soul unconquerable" (233).

It is a strange, barbaric, exciting story, and Graham tells it with gusto and with characteristic lively oscillation (rather than still balance) of judgment. He admires the courage but deplores the waste, and understands the religious aspiration but drily rebukes it—"a fine day, with health to enjoy it, is the most spiritual of the pleasures open to mankind." The result is the best of his sequence of biographies, a well-paced, climactic account. Another reason for its success is that as his main source Graham had no archaic chronicle but *Os Sertões,* the massive Brazilian prose-epic by Euclydes da Cunha.[2] Graham's debt to da Cunha is even greater than his numerous acknowledgments suggest; but, as was noted in *Cunninghame Graham: A Critical Biography* (277–78), *A Brazilian Mystic* is redeemed from the charge of plagiarism not only by Graham's selective and relatively nimble approach but also by the marked tonal shifts toward the melancholy and elegiac. Da Cunha wrote with a remorseless forensic zeal; Graham writes with wry pity for the waste of human life and effort.

Five years after the publication of *A Brazilian Mystic* appeared *Doughty Deeds,* a completely contrasting biography: an act of homage by the author to his ancestor Robert Graham of Gartmore (1735–97), the author of the poem "If doughty deeds my lady please, / Right soon I'll mount my steed."[3] As a young man, Robert

Graham had voyaged to Jamaica and there became a plantation-owner, slave-dealer, and tax-collector; in later years he returned to Scotland, inheriting the estates of Gartmore and Finlaystone, becoming Rector of Glasgow University, corresponding with Smollett, and entering Parliament as a Whig who proposed a Bill of Rights which anticipated the Great Reform Bill of 1832.

The basic material of the book is a collection of his letters; but in the rather repetitive linking commentary the biographer seems to be making a little go a long way, and a further constraint is his reluctance to intrude when Robert Graham writes to his wife, Annie. "These letters, wedged in between advices to correspondents on the 'Musquito Shore,' old bills of lading, advertisements for negroes that had run away and strictures on the policy the Governor pursued, written to various friends, I leave uncopied, holding that as a descendant of the man who wrote them, it is more consonant with 'le respect humain' to look and then pass on" (50). Nevertheless, an adequate if incomplete picture of Robert Graham emerges: a bluff, frank, businesslike man, who in a letter from Jamaica in 1760 writes:

You may possibly remember that in the days of your more early acquaintance, I was not remarkable for that cold Virtue, Chastity, but indiscriminately found my sentiments agreeable to my desires and gave rather too great a latitude to a dissipated train of whoring, the consequence of which . . . . . I now dayly see before me in a motely variegated race of different complexions. Amongst these there is a Younker by the white girl, who formerly lived with me, who is now of age to leave the Island. . . . [M]y present views are to fit him for these scenes of Life which occurr amongst people whose principal study is to make fortunes, by which means the extensive parade of Greek and Latin, etc., is avoided and the whole plan constricted into a competent knowledge of Mathematics and Mechanics. . . . . (71–72)

In such ways the book reminds us that the high civilization of the gentry in eighteenth-century Britain was largely financed by the slave trade and by the tough patriarchy of the sugar plantations. Like his biographer, Robert Graham was an enlightened man by the standards of his day; and also like his biographer, he owed to the labors of many dependants the leisure to publish his enlightened ideas.

The third of this biographical sequence, *José Antonio Páez* (1929), returns us to South America in the nineteenth century. Páez liberated Venezuela from the Spaniards after a long series of guerrilla campaigns in which he led his llaneros in lance-charges against the Spanish cavalry. Originally an illiterate ranch-hand, he became the chief ally of Bolívar in the wars of liberation, established the independence of Colombia by his brave leadership at the Battle of Carabobo, rose to be thrice President of Venezuela, and yet as an old man knew defeat and humiliation. When imprisoned by his rival Monagas, he was confined to a cell so stifling that he had to lie flat to breathe the air that came under the door; and at the age of seventy-eight, during his exile, he worked as a commission-agent for a cattle company. This was the man who in his prime had won the affection and admiration of his llaneros by his foolhardy courage in battle, bluff good humor, and rough-and-ready life-style; his troops called him *Tío,* "Uncle." Naturally keen to present this "Liberator" in a favorable light, Graham contrasts him with the more patrician and egoistic Bolívar, and gives prominence to incidents which, like the following, illustrate Páez's merciful qualities: "As he passed through the little town of Magdalena, a man fired a blunderbuss at him out of a window, so close that it singed his clothes. . . . . The would be murderer was seized at once and brought before his intended victim. Páez told him he was a miserable shot and set him free at once." (279).

As Cunninghame Graham's main sources were the autobiographical writings of Páez,[4] it is not greatly surprising that many such favorable incidents appear; but although some of them may test the reader's credulity, the general picture of Páez as, for most of his life, a popular, brave, indefatigable, and generous leader is well confirmed by other sources. The biography is patchy toward the end, when Graham deals with events not covered by Páez's memoirs, and the reader learns little of Páez's policies as president. (A subsequent historian remarks that this Páez was a dictator who curtailed the freedom of the press and "really had no constructive policies to carry out."[5]) The final impression is of a rapid, sympathetic, but not very searching book.

In 1873, steaming upstream, a Brazilian gunboat reached the town of Humaitá in Paraguay. Cunninghame Graham was a passenger. He saw the ruined church, devastated by shelling, against a background of tall and shattered palm trees and surrounded by

damaged houses: a relic of the long war which had recently laid
Paraguay waste—"an example of what the might, the majesty and
power of civilisation could accomplish."[6] Then from the Chaco shore
a canoe slid out; three of the four Indians in it were squatting,
roasting meat on a lump of clay, while their leader, with drawn
bow and arrow, scanned the stream for fish. The crew of the gunboat,
seeing the Indians, cried, *Os barbaros!* ("The barbarians!"), and would
have fired at them if they had not been restrained. Graham perceived
the ironies, and sixty years later, in *Portrait of a Dictator* (1933), he
did them justice.

The dictator in question was Francisco Solano López, who mis-
ruled Paraguay from 1865 to 1870. This fat, fanatical, and sadistic
individual inherited the powers of his father, President Carlos Antonio López, and soon exceeded the father in tyrannical excesses.
"Still, though a coward he was not a fool, unless a megalomaniac
comes under that head" (167). Hoping to emulate Napoleon and
to make Paraguay renowned through warfare, he led his nation into
a suicidal campaign against Brazil, Uruguay, and Argentina. To
Graham's perplexity, the tyrant's forces fought with remarkable
bravery and tenacity, even though, in his reign of terror, López
treated loyal followers as barbarously as enemies. He gave orders
that on the battlefields, badly wounded soldiers of his own side
were to be killed, in addition to the enemy wounded; and meanwhile
countless citizens were arrested, tortured, and executed on charges
concocted to gratify his paranoia.

As the war dragged on, the land became wasted and largely
depopulated. To provide more cannon-fodder, males between the
ages of ten and sixty were conscripted, while women between sixteen
and forty were drafted to take the men's places as laborers in the
fields. While his starving and ragged army retreated around him,
López and his retinue feasted and drank choice wines. He had had
his mother and brothers tortured, and one of his last acts was to
sign his mother's death-warrant. At last, hunted down by the Brazilian cavalry, he was lanced and fell dead in the mud. His mistress,
Madame Lynch, escaped in a coach with a store of valuables, and
later enjoyed years of fashionable luxury in Paris and London: Graham sometimes saw her, elegantly dressed, "still handsome and
distinguished looking" (272).

In the histories of the Spanish conquest, Cunninghame Graham
had been offering ironic commentary on the imperialism of his own

times; and in *Portrait of a Dictator,* his mirror of the past again reflected light on the present. In 1933, the year the book appeared, treason trials were decimating Stalin's Russia, Mussolini was considering the invasion of Abyssinia, and Adolf Hitler was appointed the Chancelor of Germany. In the following year, Hitler was proclaimed Führer; and soon would begin that World War which in its depths of evil as well.as its scale of destruction would far surpass even López's era. With hindsight, Graham's *Portrait of a Dictator* can be construed as a prophetic warning: a timely commentary on the power of a dictatorial leader, loyally served by his people, to embroil whole nations in years of carnage and destruction. Recalling South America of the 1860s, Cunninghame Graham was addressing Europe of the 1930s. His book was actually banned in Paraguay, where López was adulated. Graham remarked bitterly: "His bust defiles the dark recesses of the Tarumensian woods. So far no bust of Judas mocks Gethsemane" (xvi).

Like his previous two biographies, *Portrait of a Dictator* is erratic in plan, and repetitive; nevertheless, it is richer and somewhat sharper than they, for Graham is describing a region that he knew well, and he had met numerous eye-witnesses of López's tyranny. Consequently the book makes a satisfactory ending to a series which had abundantly illustrated Cunninghame Graham's perennial theses—that "progress" is an illusion and that "civilization" is essentially no better than barbarism.

Chapter Six
The Later Collections

The three final collections of sketches were *Redeemed* (1927), *Writ in Sand* (1932), and *Mirages* (1936). *Redeemed* contains numerous pieces which with almost facile stylishness evoke the atmosphere of a particular place and time. Examples include "Oropesa," which describes a Spanish town with a decaying church abandoned to owls and rats; "Inch Cailleach," the Island of the Nuns, mournful amid the cold waters of a Scottish loch; and "Dar el Jinoun," a great house in Morocco which once was crowded with the fashionable and the cosmopolitan, but which now stands empty: "The fountain is half full of empty sardine tins and broken glass. The fruit-trees stand neglected and unpruned. Only the palms, their heads in fire, their feet in water, flourish and raise their feathery branches, reminding one of a deserted lighthouse still keeping watch over a ruined port" (134–35).

Transience, decay, mortality. Cunninghame Graham was a virtuoso in their evocation, and never more so than in the tale "Animula Vagula." The title quotes a poem by the Emperor Hadrian which begins:

> *Animula vagula blandula*
> *Hospes comesque corporis*
> *Quae nunc abibis in loca* . . . . .
>
> (Soul of man, congenial and elusive little spirit,
> Guest and partner of the body,
> Where will you go to now?)

In the story, an orchid-hunter tells how once, in Colombia, Indians brought from the forest the corpse of an unknown white man for burial. The speaker evokes the occasion and setting with an intensity of detail, down to the stranger's worn, green leather cigarette-case edged with silver and holding just three cigarettes; and the greater the factual plenitude, the more unbreakable seems the grip of death on the young white man and his identity.

"No one had thought of closing his blue eyes; and as we are but creatures of habit after all, I put my hand into my pocket, and taking out two half-dollar pieces was about to put them on his eyes. Then I remembered that one of them was bad, and you will not believe me, but I could not put the bad piece on his eyes; it looked like cheating him. So I went out and got two little stones, and after washing them put them upon his eyelids, and at least they kept away the flies." (43)

As in D. H. Lawrence's "Odour of Chrysanthemums," a profounder yet kindred tale, the author has striven to convey the full challenge which the still opacity of the dead offers to the conventions and rituals of the living. The Commissary and his assistant formally note the young man's possessions (" 'Case, 1; cigarettes, 3' "), and the more systematic the official notation of the *fact* of death, the more imposingly arcane appears the *state*.

Finally, the orchid-hunter who has been recalling this encounter disembarks from the steamer on which he has been voyaging up-stream, and enters the jungle as though in exchange for the young man who had once been carried from it:

We waved our hands and crowded on the steamer's side, and watched him walking up the bank to where a little group of Indians stood holding a bullock with a pack upon its back.

They took his scanty property and, after tying it upon the ox, set off at a slow walk along a little path towards the jungle, with the grey figure of our late companion walking quietly along, a pace or two behind. (56–57)

The same collection contains the most famous of Cunninghame Graham's obituary tributes: "Inveni Portum" [I Have Found Harbor], an account of Conrad's funeral at Canterbury, at a time when, ironically, the city was brightly decked in bunting for the cricket festival. Another irony was that for all Conrad's bitter skepticism, a Roman Catholic service was held at the funeral: but then Conrad had seen the faith "as a bulwark against Oriental barbarism" and as an associate of Polish patriotism; and Graham remarks, "What, after all, is better for the soul than prayer to an unseen God, in an uncomprehended tongue?"

The piece movingly evokes the appearance and character of the Polish writer who for twenty-seven years had been Graham's closest literary friend. "His nose was aquiline, his eyes most luminous and full. It seemed his very soul looked out of them, piercing the thoughts of those whom he addressed; his beard, trimmed to a point, was flecked with grey a little and his moustache was full. His face, of the dull yellow hue that much exposure to the tropic sun in youth so often causes, was lined and furrowed by the weather" (167–68). This character sketch well indicates the tensions and paradoxes that generated the power of Conrad's novels:

> His cheek bones, high and jutting out a little, revealed his Eastern European origin, just as his strong square figure and his walk showed him a sailor, who never seems to find the solid earth a quite familiar footing after a sloping deck. His feet were small and delicately shaped, and his fine, nervous hands, never at rest a minute in his life, attracted you at once. They supplemented his incisive speech by indefinable slight movements. . . . . Something there was about him, both of the Court and of the quarterdeck, an air of courtesy and of high breeding, and yet with something of command. . . . .
>
> As he discoursed upon the things that interested him, recalled his personal experiences, or poured his scorn and his contempt upon unworthy motives and writers who to attain their facile triumphs had pandered to bad taste, an inward fire seemed to be smouldering ready to break out, just as the fire that so long smouldered in the hold of the doomed ship in which he made his first voyage to the East suddenly burst out into flames. (168–69)

Another obituary tribute is "Wilfrid Scawen Blunt," which evokes the old Jacobean house, Newbuildings in Sussex, where Blunt had lived like an Arab potentate, striding about in long robes, his full beard spanning his chest; proud, vain, arrogant, yet always ready to listen to tales of oppression told by the pilgrims (Arabs and Persians, Turks and Indians) who visited him there. "If he believed all that they told him is difficult to say; but possibly his passion for the liberty of down-trodden nationalities, and his hatred of imperialism, sometimes rendered him their prey" (65). Graham saw him as "a Cassandra prophesying in the wilderness," for Blunt had warned England that Egypt would one day be free, that Ireland would achieve independence, and that the Indian Empire would revolt. "Had he been listened to, the measures that have been wrung from us by force would have been graciously bestowed; but then who looks for vision in a statesman or a man of business and does not find himself deceived?" (65).

In a lyrical but rather sentimental peroration of the kind that comes almost automatically to Graham, the dead Blunt is imagined lying face upward to the stars and sensing the cycle of the seasons and the constellations—or if not, "oblivion, the best gift the gods have to bestow, will bring him peace at last."

In stark contrast, the tale "A Hundred in the Shade" is another of Cuninghame Graham's brothel-pieces; or, more precisely, another of his tales about a cultured and kind-hearted prostitute. This Daphne Villiers bears a strong resemblance to the Elise of the earlier collections: her rooms would gratify a connoisseur of the arts. "Two or three bits of china, good but inexpensive, with one fine piece of Ming, and a Rhodes plate or two were dotted here and there"; and her bookshelves contain works by Anatole France and Maupassant, Dante's *Vita Nuova,* and the *Heptameron.* She falls in love with one of her clients, who is called away on business; on his return he, the inner narrator, finds that she has gone to Tampico with a mining engineer who, she hopes, may one day marry her. The speaker falls silent. The implication is that through inhibition, convention, or bad luck (the business trip at the wrong time) he may have sacrificed both his and the girl's chance of happiness. But, as in the case of Elise, the reader may sense some incompatibility between the girl's imputed sensitivity and the rigors of her chosen profession. The tale's setting seems more plausible than its center.[1]

"Los Llanos del Apure" is an essay on the plains of Venezuela which has understandably attracted the attentions of anthology editors; for after a survey of the llaneros' lives on those vast grassy expanses, Graham embarks on what was probably his most deliberate descriptive set-piece, a rendering of the Venezuelan sky at sunset:

Green turns to mauve, then back to green again; to scarlet, orange, and vermilion, flinging the flag of Spain across the sky. Dark coffee-coloured bars, shooting across a sea of carmine, deepen to black; the carmine melts into pale grey. Castles and pyramids spring up; they turn to cities; the pyramids to broken arches, waterfalls, and ships, with poops like argosies. Gradually pale apple-green floods all the heaven; then it fades into jade. Castles and towns and ships and broken arches disappear. The sun sinks in a globe of fire, leaving the world in mourning for its death.

Then comes the after-glory, when all the colours that have united, separated, blended and broken up, unite and separate again, and once more blend. A sheet of flame, that for an instant turns the Apure into a streak of molten metal, bathes the Llano in a bath of fire, fades gradually and dies, just where the plain and sky appear to join as if the grass was all aglow. (39)

This description is labored, and it has its clichés ("floods all the heaven," "leaving the world in mourning for its death"), but it nevertheless achieves a lurid vividness.

The subsequent collection, *Writ in Sand,* is relatively sparse, compared with *Redeemed.* It includes "Tschiffely's Ride," an account (obviously based on newspaper clippings) of Aimé Tschiffely's epic ride of fifteen thousand miles from Buenos Aires to New York on two Argentine *criollo* horses, Mancha and Gato: a demonstration of the toughness of the breed. Cunninghame Graham's warm enthu-siasm for Tschiffely was soon reciprocated, and the rider became Graham's second biographer on the publication of *Don Roberto.* (The first biography of Graham, by Herbert Faulkner West, appeared in 1932, the same year as *Writ in Sand.*)

Another piece, "Fin de Race," offers rambling reminiscences of an old Spanish acquaintance, Bernardino de Velasco, Duke of Frías, whose main vocation was to waste his inheritance at gambling tables. Then there are three descriptive essays: "Writ in Sand," dealing (somewhat credulously) with a circus; "Camara de Lobos," portray-ing a religious procession in a Portuguese fishing village; and "The Stationmaster's Horse," a Paraguayan recollection. Of these, the first is relatively slight, and the second is a somewhat routine ac-count; but the third is keener—and is given a vicarious poignancy by the fact that the wild gallop in which the youthful Graham overtook a train in order to post a letter is now being recalled by a writer whose eightieth birthday fell in the year of the book's publication.

The remaining piece is " 'Creeps,' " a character study of Joseph Crawhall, the taciturn artist from Newcastle who had become res-ident in Tangier. This sympathetic recollection of the time when Crawhall was retrieved, tranquil and unembarrassed, from the local brothel, ends adroitly thus:

A few days afterwards, as we walked through the "Soko de la fuera," a blind man seated on the ground begged, raising one hand to heaven as he called upon God's name. "Creeps" gave him half a silver dollar, and when I said the man had never seen himself possessed of so much capital, broke into one of his rare smiles, that lit up his whole face, transfiguring it, as if his inner genius struggled to come forth, and answered, "I too have been blind." (95)

Mirages, the last of Cunninghame Graham's collections, appeared in the year of his death, 1936, and it makes a fine ending to his career. The Preface is one of his best, a vigorous assertion that, for all the changes he has seen in his lifetime, he feels as hostile to imperialism and as skeptical of civilization as he has ever felt. "Civilisation . . . . . to me appears to be founded on mud, cemented well with blood, and sustained precariously upon the points of bayonets" (xi–xii). "I well know that though all races of mankind may suffer outward changes, still underneath the skin all men are equal, and the best manicured Nordic variety of *Homo Sapiens,* for all his plumbing, is not really better than the bull-whacker of Haiti, or the herder of the buffalo in the marshes of Ceylon" (xiii).

In the subsequent sketches, however, the satirically polemical note is seldom heard: the older Graham has become a more mellow, tolerant person, it seems, and he now looks with sympathy on most of the beings who cross his path. "The Dream of the Magi" offers a reconstruction of the visit of the Wise Men to Jesus: there is little to trouble and much to gratify the pious. "Inmarcesible" portrays the pitiable sufferings of the horses who died during the Boer War. "Casas Viejas, 1933" reports an incident in Spain when a communistic uprising in a village was suppressed bloodily by the troops: on the whole, as one would expect, Graham's sympathies lie with the villagers. And although Graham was no lover of bull-fighting, in "Los Niños Toreros" he records with sharp observation and evident compassion the work of a limping, worried torero and his two sons at a seedy bull-ring in Caracas. This is one of his better tales, and a culmination to that long discussion of ways in which an impoverished performance may surpass an opulent one.

Although Graham was often thought of (and portrayed) as a Don Quixote tilting at windmills, quite as appropriate an image would have been that of a Hamlet—particularly the Hamlet meditating on the skull. If Graham rode with gauchos and fought for the rights of workers, he also haunted graveyards, meditating on memorials. "Up Stage" offers melancholy (and somewhat sentimental) specu-

lations about the identity of a man, perhaps an actor, who is now
known to posterity only by a name and a date on a lonely headstone
on the Isle of Bute. It was bitter to Graham, that nagging sense
that death may also mean oblivion, the sense that identities may
fade and evaporate; all his life as a writer he fought it, memorializing
again and again those he had met, whether noblemen or beggars,
heroes or rogues. For posterity he preserves the biography of Charles
Mitchell, "Charlie the Gaucho," who had returned from England
to resume a wandering life in Uruguay, only to die in a knife-fight.
His death is described with Graham's customary unflinching realism. "The man had fallen with his right arm underneath his head.
His left still was in the attitude of holding up the intestines, although the fingers were relaxed, and underneath his cotton chiripá
the lump was plainly visible where the bowels had escaped and
stained his soiled white drawers with blood" (21).

In lighter tone is "Bibi," a character-sketch of Bibi Carleton, a
raffish, randy, yet charismatic character of Tangier who, when appointed British Consular Agent at Elcazar, instituted a paternalistic
version of a protection racket among the poor farmers of the region.
And in the final piece of the book, " 'Facón Grande,' " Graham
sketches the characters of the fellow Europeans who used to band
together with him during the times of Indian uprisings in Argentina. He brings them to life deftly enough in a few lines—Don
Martin, for example, "one of our best leaders against the Indians
. . . . . , mounted on his skewbald, his rifle hanging from his
saddle"; the wind would blow back the brim of his Panama hat as
he rode from house to house along the Sauce Grande, the Sauce
Corto and Naposta, warning the neighbours to be ready to fight
(179).

Of such acquaintances, Graham says in the concluding paragraph:
"Where they ride now is but a matter of conjecture; no one remembers them but I who write these lines, that I have written *in
memoriam,* hoping that some day they will allow an old companion
to ride with them, no matter where they ride" (182). "No one
remembers them but I who write these lines": the words epitomize
Cunninghame Graham's intense combination of egotism and altru-
ism. His proud selfhood led him to bid for historic immortality by
self-commemorating works; yet those works necessarily preserved
the people, places, birds, and beasts of his bygone years and became
part of a general quest or life-project of his to strive to forestall and

sap the powers of death and oblivion. When he was dying of pneumonia in Argentina, he remarked, "Some people need religion like a wall to lean against, but I have never needed it."[2] During his lifetime, he had built his own wall: the long, irregular, and crumbling wall of his own writings.

Chapter Seven
Conclusion

Cunninghame Graham is not a major author, and if we come to his work with the wrong expectations much of it can be seen as slight, bitty, thin, and repetitive: yarns, journalism, chat, and whimsy of the past. He was only marginally a writer of fictions: his concern for the sensed truth and his partly defensive, partly aggressive project to memorialize his own career meant that he either stayed within the bounds of what he had experienced or generally restricted invention to the locations he knew. If, however, we come to his work with the right expectations—a flexible cluster of criteria based on normal human curiosity and governed by common sense—we will find much to enjoy and something to learn. We move between relatively ephemeral, trivial material and, in contrast, pieces which linger in the imagination and bear rereading, the latter group including "The Gold Fish," for example, and "A Jesuit," "Christie Christison," "Might, Majesty, and Dominion," and "Animula Vagula." A work may ask to be treated as a tale or as an autobiographical recollection, as a travel essay or as a description of some bygone custom; often, the piece may prove to be a mixture of several of these.

As we look back from *Mirages* over the tales and essays of his previous forty years, we can readily see the continuities and the degree of evolution. The later work is technically more reliable and less erratic, better paced and balanced, although Cunninghame Graham was always capable of errors and lapses in spelling, punctuation, and syntax. (We often sense the amateurism of this "amateur of genius.") The later writer is more tolerant, more forgiving in outlook; the earlier satiric scorn and ironic indignation are muted. To the last, the better pieces maintain a blend of honest realism and stoical sympathy.

The thematic continuity between earlier and later work is extremely strong. As we have seen, defense of the underdog is the main preoccupation that links Graham the political campaigner with Graham the writer. In his tales, essays, biographies, and histories, as in his parliamentary speeches, he calls into question the belief in inevitable progress and faith in imperialism, and he sympathizes with the downtrodden and the victim, whether Maori, Zulu, Mescalero Indian, Aztec, or animal—horses on battlefields or elephants performing in circuses. Prostitutes, beggars, eccentrics: where he can speak up for them, he does; at best with a dry humor and a recognition that not all have hearts of gold.

As is natural to a man who lived an active life and preferred the sunny skies of Argentina and Morocco to the dank drizzle of Scotland, a strong element of cultural and chronological primitivism accompanies his criticism of civilization: his ideal world would be a preindustrial one of virile activity in an open, hot landscape, where men ride, work, drink, and occasionally fight, living for the moment and free from the urgings of conscience and the claims of posterity. This puerile Arcadia is a familiar imaginative retreat for writers who know well those urgings and who nevertheless are too intelligently reflective ever to become domiciled in the primitive state that they commend. Graham recognized the irony. Near the end of his career he remarked: "I pray the empire builder . . . . . not to think I am enamoured of the noble savage . . . . . I know quite well that he uses no poison gas or bombs, simply because he has not got them, and is constrained to do his level best with poisoned arrows . . . . ." (*Mirages,* xii).

In this matter, as in others, his work is ambiguous and tends toward paradox. He looks on the primitive sometimes with admiration, sometimes with equanimity, and sometimes with distaste, depending on its nature, his vantage-point, and his polemical purposes. With religion, as we have noted, he has a perennial concern, and can look variously with scorn, sympathy, and approval at particular manifestations of it. Scottish missionaries he can see as misguided exporters of a dismal, life-denying creed to regions happier and better without it; Jesuits he can often admire for their heroism and paternalism in South America; gnostic fanaticism, as of Antonio Conselheiro, he can regard as a mental disease yet also as an idealism that lifts men from the mundane. Cunninghame Graham was a romantic and a skeptic: his spiritual forebears included both Shelley and Voltaire. In racial matters, he sometimes endorses the prejudices of his day, as in some patronizing or mocking reference to Jew or

Negro (in "Rothenberger's Wedding," for instance); but he can also, at his best, challenge or transcend that prejudice, as we saw in the case of "Mirahuano." His attitude to women may here and there be the rather dominative one that fits the conventional posture of the "virile man of action"; but on numerous occasions he challenges sexual chauvinism and exposes its callousness.

Cunninghame Graham was a man of paradoxes, expressing more overtly the complexities that can be found in many people who live with sufficient fullness in any cultural phase. In this century, steadily increasing critical interest has been drawn to such paradoxicality in individuals and their works: therefore Graham may attract and reward new attention.

A central paradox is that which he poses eloquently in the late essay "Mirage":

So it may well be after all that the world of the mirage is the real world, and that the world we live in is a mirage. Mankind has always loved to be deceived, to hug illusions to its heart, to fight for them and to commit its direst follies in the name of common sense . . . . .

When, therefore, fellow Hadgi, the mirage spreads its lake before you, do not allow your horse to put his foot in it or it will vanish from your sight.

Behind the mantling vapour rise castles, towers, cathedrals, lines of aerial telegraphs stretching up to the moon, palaces, fantastic ruins, galleons and galleasses that sail bedecked with flags.

All these exist in the mind's eye, the only field of vision where there is no astigmatism.

Rein up your horse, before his feet destroy and bring them back again to earth. Why peer behind the veil to see life's desert all befouled with camels' dung, littered with empty sardine tins and broken bottles, and strewed as thick as leaves in Vallombrosa with greasy, sandwich papers?

At any cost preserve your mirage intact and beautiful. If riding in the desert you behold it slowly taking shape, turn and sit sideways in your saddle, pouring a libation of tobacco smoke towards your Mecca and muttering a prayer. (*Mirages,* 6, 7, 8)

The passage is "dated"; stylistically slightly archaic for the time of writing, too. It is redolent of late-nineteenth-century romanticism by its stance, argument, tone, and phrasing ("fellow Hadgi [pilgrim] . . . . . Why peer behind the veil . . . . . ?"), which recall Fitzgerald's *Omar Khayyám* or early Yeats and the Aesthetic prose of the 1890s. At a casual glance it might pass for a wistful reverie by Arthur Symons or Richard le Gallienne, although the quirky Miltonic allusion ("leaves in Vallombrosa"[1]) offers a warning. What gives the passage its paradoxical edge is suggested by the reference to "life's desert all befouled with camels' dung, littered with empty sardine tins and broken bottles, and strewed . . . . . with greasy, sandwich papers." The essay purports to commend illusion, dream, and ideality; but these mundane references remind us that again and again Graham had been concerned with drawing attention to precisely those sardine tins, those broken bottles, those greasy sandwich papers. In all his best work, the mundane realist controls the aspiring romantic. This passage reveals, in addition, a further and greater tension.

It has recently been argued, by Professor A. D. Nuttall in *A Common Sky*, that the reason modern writers and critics place such high value on the concrete and particular in depictions of life is that they are responding to a solipsistic fear. The solipsist holds that the individual self constitutes the sole verifiable reality; our sense of an outside world is unverifiable and may be deceptive and delusive. Nuttall argues that although common sense revolts against such a notion, it is tenacious and hard to exorcise; it generates anxieties. "It is strange how many modern writers betray real anxiety in their efforts to give a rich, felt 'substance' to the things they describe . . . . . Perhaps, in short, the romantic and post-romantic stress on 'impact' is *compensatory*." "If a man feels the real world slipping from him, he tightens his grip on it."[2]

For us the application is clear. Cunninghame Graham's work, as we have seen, from time to time expresses radically skeptical and even solipsistic notions ("It may well be . . . . . that the world we live in is a mirage"), and there is something akin to a compensatory anxiety in his determination to render the concreteness of the world. "We all must put our finger in the Saviour's wounds, before we can believe," he says;[3] and he delights when the senses seem unexpectedly to provide incontrovertible guarantee of remembered reality, with a scent of mimosa suddenly recalling the River Plate, the sight of green turtle-fat evoking the Indians of Bahía Blanca, and the smell of oranges summoning the forests of Paraguay.[4] So an ontological fear may well reinforce his memorializing concern: he is striving to give fixity as well as durability to his remembered world.

Another paradoxical feature of his outlook, as we have noted from time to time in previous chapters, is the tendency for his defense of the underdog to extend itself from political into aesthetic regions, to the point where he argues that the impoverished and amateurish work may actually be more effective than the opulent and professional. In "A Repertory Theatre," the amateur production of a Spanish play seems to him more evocative than a professional treatment could be; in "Miss Christian Jean," clumsy paintings stimulate his imagination as proficient ones do not; in "Euphrasia," the poorly carved cross and cheap iron railings make the war memorial the more poignant; and among the chroniclers, it is the ex-soldier Bernal Díaz, with his honest, unpolished comments, who for Graham brings the Conquest most immediately to life. This has obvious relevance to our judgment of Graham's own pages. Cunninghame Graham's quirky awkwardnesses of style and narration, his inconsequentialities and digressions, his love of a gratuitous footnote about a horse or a Spanish phrase: all these features can, where the material purports to be autobiographical, serve as warrants of authenticity. Faults may become merits. The more Graham presents himself as a traveler and man of action turned only late to writing, the more the quirks and flaws provide confirmation. We make allowances for the lapses, and when a tale succeeds, we may give extra credit for the overcoming of conspicuous difficulties.

It is also the case that his huge and largely autobiographical output permits us to know him so fully and intimately that to be critically severe to Graham would seem as unjust as to be harsh to an old and close friend. He helped underdogs; today he himself is an underdog who deserves a little help. Much modern literary criticism perversely strives to isolate from their authors the works under discussion. With Graham's work, this is impossible. Among real-life characters, he was and is one of the most interesting; and the ample collection of tales, essays, biographies, and histories constitutes a large part of his masterpiece, warts and all: the living Cunninghame Graham.

Notes and References

Chapter One

1. Jacob Epstein, *Epstein: An Autobiography* (London: Hulton, 1955), p. 88; Arthur Symons, *Notes on Joseph Conrad* (London: Myers, 1925), p. 32; George Bernard Shaw, *Three Plays for Puritans* (London: Richards, 1911), p. 301; G. K. Chesterton, *Autobiography* (London: Hutchinson, 1936), p. 269; John Lavery, *The Life of a Painter* (London: Cassell, 1940), p. 92.

2. Vernon Lee (pseudonym of Violet Paget), *Louis Norbert: A Two-Fold Romance* (London: Lane, 1914), pp. 85–86. In 1909 Graham led a demonstration on behalf of Francisco Ferrer, a Spanish anarchist.

3. Unpublished letter, 12 February 1902, NLS.

4. Unpublished letter, William Bontine to Mrs. Katon, PC.

5. Vol. 4, p. 4.

6. See *AFT*, pp. 44–45 (capture by revolutionaries); pp. 166–68 (fencing salon); A. F. Tschiffely, *This Way Southward* (London: Hodder & Stoughton, 1941), p. 22 (capture by Indians); A. F. Tschiffely, *Tornado Cavalier* (London: Harrap, 1955), pp. 63–68 (capture by Indians).

7. Letter to Mrs. Bontine (his mother), 23 January [1873], PC.

8. Gartmore accounts for 1875–76, Scottish Record Office, Edinburgh.

9. Robert to Mrs. Bontine, 1 November 1879, PC.

10. Gabriela Cunninghame Graham, *The Christ of Toro and Other Stories* (London: Eveleigh Nash, 1908), pp. 83, 90.

11. Letter to Theodore Roosevelt, 27 March 1917, in *Redeemed* (London, 1927), p. 71.

12. *A Report of Proceedings* (privately printed, 1884), p. 4, NLS.

13. *Vanity Fair,* 5 February 1887, p. 87.

14. *Hansard's Parliamentary Debates,* Series 3, Vol. 331, column 733 (1 December 1888). Sergius Saranoff says "Withdraw! Never!" in *Arms and the Man,* Act 3.

15. *Hansard,* 6 March 1889, col. 1089.

16. A. Briggs and J. Saville, eds., *Essays in Labour History 1886–1923* (London: Macmillan, 1971), 2:45.

17. Emrys Hughes, *Keir Hardie* (London: Allen & Unwin, 1956), p. 33.

18. Unpublished letters of 24 October 1887 and 24 May 1887, PC.

19. William Stewart, *J. Keir Hardie: A Biography* (London: Cassell, 1921), p. 22.

20. Engels: Yvonne Kapp, *Eleanor Marx* (London: Lawrence & Wishart, 1976), 2:226. Graham: letter to *Christian Socialist* (London) 6 (January 1888):13.

21. *Times*, 14 November 1887, pp. 6–7; *Scotsman*, 14 November 1887, p. 7; *Glasgow Herald*, 23 November 1887, p. 9. Some reports give Blunden's name as Blundell.

22. William Kent, *John Burns: Labour's Lost Leader* (London: Williams & Norgate, 1950), p. 30.

23. *Times*, 14 November 1887, p. 9.

24. Wilfrid Scawen Blunt, *My Diaries*, part 2 (London: Secker, 1920), p. 197.

25. *WD*, pp. 230–33.

26. Ibid., p. 241.

27. Ibid., p. 244.

28. *Scots Independent*, July 1931, supplement, p. 2.

29. Sherry, *Conrad's Western World* (London: Cambridge University Press, 1971), p. 149.

30. M. M. Mahood, *The Colonial Encounter* (London: Collings, 1977), p. 32.

31. H. G. Wells, *When the Sleeper Wakes* (London & New York: Harper, 1899), p. 19.

32. Undated letter (probably of 1910) and another of 24 April 1907, NLS.

33. I transcribed the letter at Graham's home (Ardoch) in 1963.

34. *JCL*, p. 64.

35. George Moore, *Conversations in Ebury Street* (London: Heinemann, 1930), pp. 159–66.

36. Letters of 5 August 1876, 23 January n.y., and 17 June n.y., PC.

37. Letter of 28 November 1890 (MS: NLS). Graham told the editor of the *Daily Graphic*: "I had hoped that the matchless pen of Bret Harte would have raised a protest against the doings in Dakota; if the protest had been made it would have run through the American Press like wildfire . . . . ." (*HFW*, pp. 85–86).

38. Letter to Garnett, 1 March 1899 (MS: University of Texas). *Mirages* (London, 1936), p. xiv.

Chapter Two

1. *The Nail and Chainmakers* (London, [1889?]), pp. 102–3.

2. *Labour Elector* (London), 15 February 1890, p. 108.

3. *Economic Evolution* (London and Aberdeen, 1891), pp. 16–17. This text frequently varies from that in *Success:* Graham polished the later version.

4. *The Imperial Kailyard* (London, 1896), pp. 7, 13–14, 14–15.

5. *JCL,* p. 87. Garnett, Introduction to Graham's *Thirty Tales and Sketches* (London, 1929), p. v.

6. Text from *Social-Democrat,* pp. 104, 108, 109. The text in *The Ipané* and subsequent collections contains numerous variants in phrasing. Partly a response to the advice of Conrad and Garnett, these revisions prove the deliberation of some, at least, of Graham's work.

7. *Notes on the District of Menteith* (London, 1895), pp. 25, 11, 12–13, 12.

8. Mr. Graham Greene kindly confirmed this fact in a letter to me dated 6 November 1980.

9. *Aurora la Cujiñi* (London, 1898), p. 13. The subsequent quotation is on p. 22. Graham revised this text considerably for later publication.

10. Symons: undated letter of 1898 (MS: NLS); Garnett: *JCL,* p. 96; Conrad: *JCL,* p. 94.

11. *JCL,* p. 86.

12. MSS transcribed by me at Graham's home, Ardoch, in 1963. Most of the Garnett/Graham correspondence is now at the University of Texas.

13. G. B. Shaw, *Three Plays for Puritans* (London: Constable, 1911), pp. 302–3.

14. Ian Maclaren, *Beside the Bonnie Brier Bush* (London: Hodder & Stoughton, 1895), p. 39.

15. *JCL,* p. 104.

16. Edward Garnett, Introduction to *Thirty Tales and Sketches* (London, 1929), p. vi.

17. *Success* (London, 1902), p. 159; *Doughty Deeds* (London, 1925), p. 42.

18. Stephen Graham, *The Death of Yesterday* (London: Benn, 1930), p. 40.

19. *Spectator,* 24 June 1899, pp. 886–87; *Literature,* 27 October 1900, p. 325; *Academy,* 29 April 1899, pp. 479–80; *Literature,* ibid.; *Speaker,* 10 November 1900, p. 164; *Academy,* 13 October 1900, pp. 301–2; *Saturday Review,* 29 April 1899, p. 533.

20. *Review of Reviews* 12 (December 1895):561.

21. Conrad: *JCL,* p. 109; Bloomfield: Introduction to *The Essential R. B. Cunninghame Graham* (London, 1952), p. 24; Haymaker: *RH,* p. 35.

22. Quoted in Jeffrey Meyers, *A Fever at the Core* (London: London Magazine Editions, 1976), p. 121.

23. *Academy,* 4 February 1899, pp. 153–54.

24. *Times,* 5 May 1898, p. 7.

25. The document is among the Harden papers.

26. Shaw, *Three Plays for Puritans*, p. 301.

27. The questionnaire is at the Academic Center Library, University of Texas.

28. Shaw, *Three Plays for Puritans*, p. 303.

Chapter Three

1. *Observer*, 20 July 1980, p. 29.

2. For example, by George Pendle in *Paraguay* (London: Oxford University Press, 1967), pp. 9–10, and by Philip Caraman in *The Lost Paradise* (London: Sidgwick & Jackson, 1975), pp. 13–14.

3. On lack of independence: C. H. Haring, *The Spanish Empire* (London: Oxford University Press, 1947), pp. 287–88; C. R. Boxer, *Salvador de Sá* (London: Athlone Press, 1952), p. 127; E. R. Service and H. S. Service, *Tobatí: Paraguayan Town* (Chicago: University of Chicago Press, 1954), pp. 35–36; resistance to decrees: H. G. Warren, *Paraguay: An Informal History* (Norman: University of Oklahoma Press, 1949), p. 98; trickery and capture: Warren, *Paraguay*, p. 90.

4. William Robertson, *Works* (London: Whitmore and Fenn, 1824), 8:79; W. H. Prescott, *History of the Conquest of Mexico* (London: Routledge, 1878), 1:542.

5. Introduction to Bernal Díaz, *The Conquest of New Spain* (Harmondsworth: Penguin, 1963), p. 12.

6. *Nation*, 1 May 1915, p. 150.

7. D. H. Lawrence, review of *Pedro de Valdivia*, *Calendar* 3 (January 1922):322–26.

Chapter Four

1. Letter of 23 June 1898, transcribed by me at Ardoch in 1963.

2. See also J. Walker, "Oscar Wilde and Cunninghame Graham," *Notes and Queries*, February 1976, pp. 73–74.

3. *JCL*, p. 99.

4. *His People* (London, 1906), p. xiii.

Chapter Five

1. *A Brazilian Mystic* (London, 1920), pp. vii–ix.

2. Da Cunha's book was first published in Río de Janeiro in 1902. A close English translation is Samuel Putnam, *Rebellion in the Backlands* (Chicago: Putnam, 1944).

3. The poem became well known through its inclusion in the popular Victorian anthology *The Golden Treasury*, edited by F. T. Palgrave. In the Everyman Edition (London: Dent, 1906) it appears on pp. 131–32.

4. J. A. Páez, *Autobiografía del General Páez* (New York: Hallet & Breen, 1867–69) and *Memorias del General José Antonio Páez* (Madrid: Editorial América, 1916).

5. J. Fred Rippy, "The Dictators of Venezuela," in *South American Dictators*, ed. A. Curtis Wilgus (New York: Russell, 1963), p. 400. Rippy remarks: "Cunninghame Graham, though always interesting, is rather unreliable" (400, footnote).

6. *Portrait of a Dictator* (London, 1933), pp. 219–20; quotation from p. 220.

Chapter Six

1. The sensitive and generous courtesan is, of course, a stock figure in novels and operas of the nineteenth and early twentieth centuries: in, for example, Dumas's *La Dame aux camélias*, Verdi's *La Traviata*, Puccini's *La Bohème*, and Conrad's *The Arrow of Gold*.

2. *AFT*, p. 437.

Chapter Seven

1. John Milton, *Paradise Lost*, Book 1, lines 302–3: "Thick as Autumnal Leaves that strow the Brooks / In *Vallombrosa*."

2. A. D. Nuttall, *A Common Sky* (London: Sussex University Press, 1974), pp. 146, 262.

3. *Mirages*, p. 5.

4. *Thirteen Stories*, pp. 215–16; *H*, p. 30; *Writ in Sand*, pp. xii–xiii.

Selected Bibliography

PRIMARY SOURCES

1. Books

Notes on the District of Menteith, for Tourists and Others. London: Black, 1895.

Father Archangel of Scotland, and Other Essays. (With Gabriela Cunninghame Graham.) London: Black, 1896.

Mogreb-el-Acksa: A Journey in Morocco. London: Heinemann, 1898.

The Ipané. London: Fisher Unwin, 1899.

Thirteen Stories. London: Heinemann, 1900.

A Vanished Arcadia: Being Some Account of the Jesuits in Paraguay, 1607 to 1767. London: Heinemann, 1901.

Success. London: Duckworth, 1902.

Hernando de Soto: Together with an Account of One of His Captains, Gonçalo Silvestre. London: Heinemann, 1903.

Progress, and Other Sketches. London: Duckworth, 1905.

His People. London: Duckworth, 1906.

Faith. London: Duckworth, 1909.

Hope. London: Duckworth, 1910.

Charity. London: Duckworth, 1912.

A Hatchment. London: Duckworth, 1913.

Bernal Díaz del Castillo: Being Some Account of Him, Taken from His True History of the Conquest of New Spain. London: Nash, 1915.

Brought Forward. London: Duckworth, 1916.

A Brazilian Mystic: Being the Life and Miracles of Antonio Conselheiro. London: Heinemann, 1920.

Cartagena and the Banks of the Sinú. London: Heinemann, 1920.

The Conquest of New Granada: Being the Life of Gonzalo Jiménez de Quesada. London: Heinemann, 1922.

The Conquest of the River Plate. London: Heinemann, 1924.

Doughty Deeds: An Account of the Life of Robert Graham of Gartmore, Poet and Politician, 1735–1797, Drawn from His Letter-Books and Correspondence. London: Heinemann, 1925.

Pedro de Valdivia, Conqueror of Chile. London: Heinemann, 1926.

Redeemed, and Other Sketches. London: Heinemann, 1927.

124

José Antonio Páez. London: Heinemann, 1929.

The Horses of the Conquest. London: Heinemann, 1930.

Writ in Sand. London: Heinemann, 1932.

Portrait of a Dictator: Francisco Solano López (Paraguay, 1865–1870). London: Heinemann, 1933.

Mirages. London: Heinemann, 1936.

2. Pamphlets and Booklets

The Nail and Chainmakers. (With J. L. Mahon and C. A. V. Conybeare.) London: London Press Agency, n.d. (probably 1889).

Economic Evolution. Aberdeen: James Leatham; London: William Reeves, 1891. Republished as *An Irish Industrial Revival.* N.p.: Socialist Party of Ireland, n.d.

The Imperial Kailyard, Being a Biting Satire on English Colonisation. London: Twentieth Century Press, 1896.

Aurora la Cujiñi: A Realistic Sketch in Seville. London: Smithers, 1898.

The Dream of the Magi. London: Heinemann, 1923.

Inveni Portam [sic]: Joseph Conrad. Cleveland, Ohio: The Rowfant Club, 1924.

Bibi. London: Heinemann, 1929.

With the North-West Wind. Berkeley Heights, N.J.: Oriole Press, 1934.

Two Letters on an Albatross. By W. H. Hudson and R. B. Cunninghame Graham. Hanover, N.H.: Westholm, 1955.

Three Fugitive Pieces. Hanover, N.H.: Westholm, 1960.

3. Selections from Material Previously Appearing in Book Form

Scottish Stories. London: Duckworth, 1914.

Thirty Tales and Sketches. (Selected by Edward Garnett.) London: Duckworth, 1929.

Rodeo. (Selected by A. F. Tschiffely.) London: Heinemann, 1936.

The Essential R. B. Cunninghame Graham. (Selected by Paul Bloomfield.) London: Cape, 1952.

Selected Short Stories. (Selected by Clover Pertíñez.) Madrid: Alhambra, 1959.

The South American Sketches of R. B. Cunninghame Graham. (Selected by John Walker.) Norman: University of Oklahoma Press, 1978.

"Beattock for Moffat" and the Best of R. B. Cunninghame Graham. (Selected by Alanna Knight.) Edinburgh: Harris, 1979.

Selected Writings of Cunninghame Graham. (Selected by Cedric Watts.) London, Toronto, and East Brunswick: Associated University Presses, 1981.

4. Translations by Cunninghame Graham

Gustavo Barroso: *Mapirunga.* London: Heinemann, 1924.

The Madonna of the Sea: a translation of Santiago Rusiñol's play *La Verge del Mar.* Unpublished, but performed at Norwich, England, in 1958.

SECONDARY SOURCES

Curle, Richard, ed. *W. H. Hudson's Letters to R. B. Cunninghame Graham.* London: Golden Cockerel Press, 1941. Letters written between 1890 and 1922 by the fellow writer and naturalist who, like Graham, had spent much of his early life in South America.

Davies, Laurence. "Cunninghame Graham's South American Sketches." *Comparative Literature Studies* 9 (September 1972):253–65.

————. "R. B. Cunninghame Graham: The Kailyard and After." *Studies in Scottish Literature* 11 (January 1974):156–77. Sophisticated critical discussions by the coauthor of *Cunninghame Graham: A Critical Biography* (listed under Watts). The former essay argues that Graham's South American pieces often have a subtler artistry than may at first be apparent; and the latter shows that the Scottish pieces were written partly in reaction against the smug insularity of the Kailyard school.

Galsworthy, John. *Forsytes, Pendyces and Others.* London: Heinemann, 1935. The brief, sympathetic discussion of Graham's character and writings emphasizes his "knight-errantry."

Garnett, Edward. "An Ironist's Outlook." *Academy and Literature* 63 (25 October 1902):436–37. A good representative of the influential early reviews of Graham by the sensitive and enthusiastic Garnett, who praised Graham's blend of pungent realism and subtle compassion.

Graham, Stephen. *The Death of Yesterday.* London: Benn, 1930. Claims that Cunninghame Graham is admirably critical when writing of Scotland but sadly sentimental when writing of Spain.

Haymaker, Richard E. *Prince-Errant and Evocator of Horizons: A Reading of R. B. Cunninghame Graham.* Kingsport, Tenn.: privately printed, 1967. An admirable labor of love: a richly detailed discussion of the themes and ideas of Graham's œuvre.

Lawrence. D. H. "*Pedro de Valdivia* by R. B. Cunninghame Graham." *Calendar* 3 (January 1927):322–26. (Reprinted in *Phoenix.* London: Heinemann, 1936.) A fierce attack on the Conquistadores for their cruelty and on their chronicler, Graham, for his egotism, casualness, and imperception.

Shaw, George Bernard. "Notes to *Captain Brassbound's Conversion.*" In *Three Plays for Puritans.* London: Richards, 1901. These notes include the witty, epigrammatic celebration of Graham's character by Shaw, who had based the play on *Mogreb-el-Acksa.*

Smith, James Steel. "R. B. Cunninghame Graham as a Writer of Short

Fiction." *English Literature in Transition* 12 (1969):61–75. A sophisticated analysis which suggests that many of Graham's short pieces, by their emphasis on loss, defeat, and arbitrary violence and by their fragmentation of experience, may have greater relevance for today's readers than for the original ones.

Stallman, R. W. "Robert Cunninghame Graham's South American Sketches." *Hispania* 28 (February 1945):69–75. Emphasizes the romantic qualities of Graham's outlook and prose techniques.

Tschiffely, A. F. *Don Roberto: Being the Account of the Life and Works of R. B. Cunninghame Graham 1852–1936.* London: Heinemann, 1937. An enthusiastic but sometimes unreliable biography presenting Graham as a swashbuckling adventurer, wit, and gallant *hidalgo.*

Walker, John. "Robert Bontine Cunninghame Graham: Gaucho Apologist and Costumbrist of the Pampa." *Hispania* 53 (1970):102–6. "As a *costumbrist* and a painter of the gaucho *modo de ser,* [Graham] approaches Hernández and Lynch, and surpasses Güiraldes in many ways," this essay suggests.

Watts, Cedric T., ed. *Joseph Conrad's Letters to R. B. Cunninghame Graham.* London: Cambridge University Press, 1969. Has an introductory discussion of this literary friendship.

———, and Davies, Laurence. *Cunninghame Graham: A Critical Biography.* London: Cambridge University Press, 1979. Planned as the first scholarly, fully documented critical biography of Graham.

West, Herbert Faulkner. *A Modern Conquistador: Robert Bontine Cunninghame Graham: His Life and Works.* London: Cranley and Day, 1932. The pioneering biography which celebrated Graham as rebel against convention and foe to Victorianism.

Index

Academy, The, quoted, 57, 62
Aestheticism, 2, 45, 55, 64, 116
Albemarle Magazine, 37
Alcibiades, 54, 82
Anarchism, 35–36
Ardoch, 6, 15, 66
Argentina, 4–5, 9–11, 47, 50,
    51, 78, 88–89, 93, 104, 113
Asquith, Herbert, 21, 29
Aztecs, 76–77, 115

Bahía Blanca, 30
Bainbridge, Tom, 30
Barnard, T. J., 26
Barrie, J. M., 48
Bax, Belfort, 41
Bazán, *see* Pardo Bazán
Beardsley, Aubrey, 45
Beerbohm, Max, 29
Bible, 30
Blacks, 78, 92–93, 115–16
Blake, William, 83
"Bloody Sunday", 5, 20–21
Bloomfield, Paul, 16, 59
Blunden, P. C., 21
Blunt, W. S., 29, 59, 108–109
Bolívar, Simón, 7, 103
Bontine, Major William, 5–6,
    7–8, 29
Bontine, Mrs. A. E., 7, 14, 29
Boswell, James, 55
Brazil, 99

Buenos Aires, 43
Buffalo Bill (William Cody), 3,
    15, 29
Burckhardt, J. L., 59
Burgess, Anthony, quoted, 70
Burns, John, 4, 18, 21, 29
Burton, Sir Richard, 70;
    Pilgrimage, 64
Butler, Samuel, 47

Cáceres, 79
Camus, Albert, 99
Carlyle, Thomas, 20, 30, 36
Carpenter, Edward, 19, 21
Casement, Roger, 29
Cayser, Sir Charles, 23
Cervantes, 48, 54, 58; *Don
    Quixote,* 3, 9, 20, 30, 58, 81,
    111
Chaucer, Geoffrey, 30, 58
Chesterton, G. K., quoted, 2
Churchill, Winston, 22
Clerici, Enrique (Enrico), 96
Cody, William, (Buffalo Bill), 3,
    15, 29
Cohen, J. M., quoted, 77
Colombia, 81
Conrad, Joseph, 3, 4, 16, 28, 29,
    38, 45, 46, 47, 58, 59, 92,
    97, 98, 107–108; letters
    quoted, 4, 29, 38, 45, 59;

WORKS:
Heart of Darkness, 48, 92, 97
"Informer, The", 27
Inheritors, The, 27
Nigger of the "Narcissus", The, 28
Nostromo, 26, 27, 94, 98
"Outpost of Progress, An", 4
Secret Agent, The, 28
Shadow-Line, The, 97

Córdoba, 10
Cortés, Hernando (Hernán), 36, 69, 76, 80
Cossart, Louis, 89
Cradley Heath, 36–37
Crawhall, Joseph, 110–11
Crockett, S. R., 48
Cunha, Euclydes da: *Os Sertões,* 101
Cunninghame Graham, Admiral Sir Angus, 13
Cunninghame Graham, Charles, 13, 23
Cunninghame Graham, Gabriela, 14–15, 17, 22, 23, 26, 41, 45
Cunninghame Graham, Malise, 13–14
Cunninghame Graham, Robert Bontine: Life: ancestry, 6–8; birth, 5–6; claim to British throne, 2, 6–7, 39–40; education, 8–9; marriage, 14; political career, 16–25; travels, 9–15, 25–26. Literary influence on others: Conrad, 26, 27; Galsworthy, 27; Greene, 44; Hueffer, 27; Masefield, 28; Shaw, 27; Wells, 27–28. Literary influences on him: 30–32, 57–58. Literary techniques: 34–36, 43–44, 46–47, 48–50, 52, 55–58, 83–84, 85, 87, 92, 96–97, 114, 118. Theme of prostitution: 91–92, 109, 115, 123

WORKS:
"Anastasio Lucena", 93, 94, 95, 98; quoted, 94
"Animula Vagula", 106–107; quoted, 107
"At Torfaieh", 47
"At Utrera", 83
"Beattock for Moffat", 82
"Belly-God, A", 94–95; quoted, 95
Bernal Díaz, 68, 76–77; quoted, 76–77
"Bibi", 112
"Bismillah", 94
" 'Bloody Niggers' ", 38–39, 47; quoted, 39
"Bolas, The", 47
"Bopicuá", 23, 96; quoted, 96
Brazilian Mystic, A, 99–101; quoted, 100, 101
"Bristol Fashion", 47–48; quoted, 48
"Brought Forward", 95
Brought Forward, 95–96
"Buta", 91
"Camara de Lobos", 110
"Captive, The", 28
Cartagena, 81
"Casas Viejas, 1933", 111
"Castles in the Air", 82
Charity, 91–92
"Charlie the Gaucho", 112; quoted, 112
"Christie Christison", 91, 92, 114
Conquest of New Granada, The, 68, 74–75; quoted, 74–75
Conquest of the River Plate, The, 68, 77, 78–79

"Creeps", 110–11; quoted, 110–11

"Dar el Jinoun", 106; quoted, 106

Doughty Deeds, 101–102; quoted, 102

"Dream of the Magi, The", 30, 111

"Dutch Smith", 91

Economic Evolution, 36, 37–38; quoted, 37

"El Babor", 42

"El Jehad", 99

"El Rodeo", 93; quoted, 93

"El Tango Argentino", 96; quoted, 96

"Elysium", 95

"Euphrasia", 118

"Evolution of a Village, The", 37

"Facón Grande", 112; quoted, 112

Faith, 91–92

"Falkirk Tryst", 94

"Fate", 87; quoted, 87

"Father Archangel of Scotland", 99

Father Archangel of Scotland, 41–44

"Feast Day in Santa Maria Mayor", 96

"Fin de Race", 110

"Fourth Magus, The", 30, 99

"Fraudesia Magna", 47

"Gold Fish, The", 52, 58, 114

"Grey Kirk, The", 87

"Gualeguaychú", 86–87; quoted, 87

"Hatchment, A", 95, 97

Hatchment, A, 93–95

"Heather Jock", 50, 51; quoted, 51

"Hegira, A", 52, 52–53

Hernando de Soto, 68, 75–6, 80; quoted, 75

"Higginson's Dream", 51–52

His People, 86–91

"His Return", 86

Hope, 91–93

Horses of the Conquest, The, 68, 77, 79–80

"Horses of the Pampas, The", 41–42

"Hundred in the Shade, A", 109; quoted, 109

"Impenitent Thief, The", 30

Imperial Kailyard, The, 36, 38; quoted, 8, 9, 38

"In a Backwater", 96

"In a German Tramp", 51

"In the Tarumensian Woods", 42

"Inch Cailleach", 106

"Inmarcesible", 111

"Inveni Portum", 107–108; quoted, 107–108

"Ipané, The", 98

Ipané, The, 5, 38, 46–51, 57, 98

Irish Industrial Revival, An, 37

"Jesuit, A", 42–43, 58, 114; quoted, 42–43

José Antonio Páez, 103; quoted, 103

"La Alcaldesa", 91

"La Clemenza di Tito", 51, 53–4; quoted, 54

"La Pulperia", 52

"Laroch, The", 86, 87

"Lazo, The", 47

"Le Chef ", 86–87, 88–89; quoted, 88–89

"London", 82

"Loose and Broken Men", 94

"Los Indios", 11, 93

"Los Llanos del Apure", 109–110; quoted 109–110

"Los Niños Toreros", 76

"Los Pingos", 23, 96

"Los Seguidores", 84–85

"McKechnie *v.* Scaramanga", 85–86

"Memory of Parnell, A", 87–88; quoted, 87–88

"Might, Majesty, and Dominion", 84, 114; quoted, 84

"Mirage", 116–17; quoted, 116

Mirages, 106, 111–12, 115; quoted, 33, 111, 115

"Mirahuano", 92–93, 115–16; quoted, 93

"Miss Christian Jean", 89–90, 118; quoted, 90

"Mist in Menteith", 94

Mogreb-el-Acksa, 27, 34, 58–67, 68; quoted, 60, 61–62, 63–64, 65

"Moral Victory, A", 95

Nail and Chainmakers, The, 36–37; quoted, 36–37

Notes on the District of Menteith, 11, 34, 39–41; quoted, 40

"Open Letter to Prince Krapotkine, An", 35–36; quoted, 35–36, 37

"Page of Pliny, A", 94

"Pakeha, A", 51–52

Pedro de Valdivia, 68, 77–78

"Pollybaglan", 86

Portrait of a Dictator, 103–105; quoted, 104, 105

"Postponed", 82–83

Preface to *The Canon,* 27

"Progress", 99

Progress, 85–86

"Pyramid, The", 84

Redeemed, 106–110

"Repertory Theatre, A", 76, 118

"Retrospect, A", 93

Rodeo, 38

"Rothenberger's Wedding", 51, 53, 115–16; quoted, 53

"San José", 9

"Sebastianist, A", 99

"Sidi bu Zibbala", 51

"Signalled", 86

"Snow in Menteith", 86, 87

"Sohail", 51

"S.S. *Atlas*", 46–7, 50, 51, 83; quoted, 51

"Stationmaster's Horse, The", 110

"Success", 39, 82

Success, 37, 82–85

"Sursum Corda", 85; quoted, 85

"Survival, A", 49, 50; quoted, 49

"Tanger la Blanca", 47

"Terror", 83

Thirteen Stories, 51–55, 56, 57

Thirty Tales and Sketches, 38

"Tobar na Reil", 87

"Traveller, A", 86

"Tschiffely's Ride", 110

"Un Angelito", 50, 57; quoted, 50, 57

"Un Autre Monsieur", 91, 98

"Un Infeliz", 85

"Un Monsieur", 91, 98

"Uno dei Mille", 95

"Up Stage", 111–12

"Upwards", 99

Vanished Arcadia, A, 42, 68–73, 81; quoted, 69, 70, 70–71, 72

"Vanishing Race, A", 42; quoted, 10–11

"Vestal, A", 80

"Victory", 52
"Wilfrid Scawen Blunt", 108–109; quoted, 108–109
"With the North-East Wind", quoted, 24
"With the North-West Wind", 47
"Writ in Sand", 110
Writ in Sand, 106, 110
"Yorkshire Tragedy, A", 86

Daily Graphic, 31, 35
Dante Alighieri, 30
Davies, Dr. Laurence, 126; quoted, 3, 85, 89
Davies, W. H., 46
Defoe, Daniel, 56, 76
Díaz, Bernal: *Verdadera historia,* 30, 76–77, 78, 118
Dickens, Charles, 20, 30, 36, 37
Donne, John, 30
Doughty, C. M., 59; *Arabia Deserta,* 64
Dowson, Ernest, 45

Ebelot, Alfred: *La Pampa,* 32
Elise, 29, 91, 97–98, 109
Engels, Friedrich, 3, 18, 19–20, 29
English Review, The, 29
Entre Ríos, 9, 10, 11
Epstein, Jacob, 1, 27, 29

Feminism, 22
Ferrer y Guardia, Francisco, 3
Fitzgerald, Edward: *Omar Khayyám,* 30, 116
Flaubert, Gustave, 28
Fleeming, Charles, 7
Ford, Ford Madox, 4, 29; *Inheritors, The,* 27; *Mr. Fleight,* quoted, 4
Fourmies, 19
Furniss, Harry, 29

Galsworthy, John, 3, 4, 27, 29, 46, 126; *Patrician, The,* 27
Garcilaso, Inca, 75
Garnett, Constance, 58
Garnett, Edward, 29, 33, 35, 45, 46, 52, 58, 62, 63, 83, 92, 126; quoted, 28, 38, 45, 46–47, 62, 83
Gartmore, 6, 15–16, 22, 23, 39, 55, 89–90
Gómara (López de Gómara), Francisco, 76
Góngora (Caballero y Góngora), Antonio, 78
Gosse, Edmund, 76
Graff, F. W. Up de, 29
Graham, Nicol, 7
Graham, Robert, ("Doughty Deeds"), 29, 101–102
Graham, Stephen: *Death of Yesterday,* 126; quoted, 57
Grahame, Robert, 7
Grahame, Sir John, 7
Greene, Graham, 44, 121n8
Gualeguaychú, 10, 86–87
Gulliver, E. H., 8

Hardie, J. Keir, 3, 17, 19, 22, 24, 29
Hardy, Thomas, 29, 95, 99
Harris, Frank, 22, 29
Harrow (School), 8
Harte, Bret, 30–32, 120n37
Harvey, Martin (later Martin-Harvey, Sir John), 29
Haymaker, R. E., 59, 126
Hernández, José: *Martín Fierro,* 30
Hitler, Adolf, 105
Holinshed, Raphael: *Chronicles,* 7
Huber, Charles, 59
Hudson, W. H., 29, 32, 38, 46, 80

Hueffer, F. M., *see* Ford, Ford
  Madox
Hughes, Emrys, 17
Hume, David, 30
Hyndman, H. M., 19, 21, 22,
  29, 34

Iceland, 47
Imperialism, 23, 38–39, 68–81
Impressionism, 52, 57–58, 83–
  84, 94
Inchmahome, 2, 6, 23
Indians: Mexican, 14–15, 52–53,
  115; North American, 14, 31–
  32, 35; South American, 11,
  12, 71–72, 74-75, 78, 79, 80,
  104, 117

James, Henry, 3, 29, 92; quoted,
  4
Jamieson, G. A., 13; quoted, 13
Jesuits, 43, 44, 70–73
Jews, 65, 96, 115–16
Jiménez, Dōna Catalina Alessan-
  dro de, 7
John, Augustus, 28
Jones, Henry Arthur, 29
Jonson, Ben, 30
Jordán, López, 9
Justice, 22, 34

Kaid of Kintafi, 59, 61–62
Kailyard School, 48–49
Kinglake, A. W.: *Eothen,* 64, 65,
  66
Kingston, William: "Rambles of
  Tom Bainbridge", 9, 30;
  quoted, 9
Kingston's Annual for Boys, 9
Kipling, Rudyard, 39, 46, 47,
  48, 53, 58, 92
Kropotkin, Prince Pyotr, 18, 29,
  35, 37

Labour Elector, The, 19, 34, 35,
  36
Labour Leader, The, 22, 34
Labour Party, 18, 22, 24, 33, 35
Labour Prophet, The, 34
Larkin, Jim, 29
Las Casas, Bartolomé de, 30
Lavery, John, 27, 28, 67; quoted,
  2
Lawrence, D. H., 46, 47, 77–78,
  83, 107, 126
Lawrence, T. E., 2, 29, 59
Lee, Vernon, (Paget, Violet): *Louis
  Norbert,* quoted, 3
Liberal Party, 16, 17, 18, 24, 35
Linklater, Eric, 24
Literature, quoted, 57
Liverpool, 22, 35
Lombroso, Cesare, 28
López, Francisco Solano, 55, 104–
  105

MacDiarmid, Hugh, (Grieve,
  C. M.), 16, 24
MacDonald, J. Ramsay, 2, 29
MacGregor, Rob Roy, 7
Maciel, Antonio, 99–101
Mackenzie, Compton, 24
Mackenzie, Henry: *Man of Feeling,
  The,* 89
Maclaren, Ian, (Watson, J.), 48,
  49; quoted, 49
Mansel, G. M., 13, 30, 94, 95,
  97, 98
Markham, Sir Clements: *Conquest
  of New Granada, The,* 73–74
Marx, Karl, 19–20, 36
Mary, Queen of Scots, 6, 82
Masefield, John, 28, 29
Maupassant, Guy de, 28, 30, 58,
  92, 109
Menteith district, 39
Menteith, Lake of, 6

Mexico, 11, 14, 77
Milton, John, 117
Montevideo, 9
Montezuma II, 76
Moore, George, 30
Morocco, 27, 51, 52, 59–67
Morris, William, 19, 20, 21, 29,
    34, 36, 37–38, 47; *News from
    Nowhere,* 20
Mussolini, Benito, 25, 105

Nation, The, quoted, 77
New Age, The, 29; quoted, 91
Nordau, Max: 28; *Degeneration,* 28
Núñez, Alvar, 69, 78, 79
Nuttall, Prof. A. D.: *Common Sky,
    A,* quoted, 117

Páez, José Antonio, 7, 103
Palgrave, F. T.: *Golden Treasury,
    The,* 30
Palgrave, Gifford, 59
Pall Mall Gazette, 29, 34
Páncharo (Pájaro), Pablo, 29, 97
Paraguay, 12–13, 43, 47, 68,
    70–73, 103–105, 117
Paralelo, Miguel, 29
Pardo Bazán, Emilia, 45
Park, Mungo, 30
Parnell, Charles, 18, 29, 54, 85,
    87–88
Pater, Walter, 47, 64
People's Press, The, 18, 19, 34;
    quoted, 19–20
Pérez Triana, Don Santiago, 94
Pizarro, Francisco, 69
Pope, Alexander, 30
Pound, Ezra, 29
Prescott, W. H., 73
Prodgers, C. H., 29

Quesada, Gonzalo Jiménez de,
    74–75

Raleigh, Sir Walter, 3, 9, 54, 82
Reid, Mayne, 9
Review of Reviews, The, quoted, 57
Rimbaud, Arthur, 30
Río de Oro, 66
Rivera, Primo de, 25
Robert I, King of Scots, 2, 6
Robert II, 6–7
Robert III, 7
Robertson, Willliam, 73
Rohlfs, Friedrich, 59
Rojas, Fernando de: *La Celestina,*
    30
Rothenstein, William, 23, 27,
    28, 60
Rusiñol (Rusinel), Santiago: *La
    Verge del Mar,* 32

Salisbury, Lord, quoted, 64
Salt, H. S., 29
Santa Teresa, 69
Saturday Review, 22, 29, 34, 46,
    47; quoted, 57
Savoy, The, 45
Scott, Sir Walter, 7
Scottish Labour Party, 18
Scottish National Party, 24–25
Scottish Nationalism, 16, 24–25
Shakespeare, William, 30, 36,
    66; *Hamlet,* 30, 111
Shaw, George Bernard, 3, 4, 18–
    19, 21, 27, 29, 48, 52, 66–
    67; *Arms and the Man,* 16, 27;
    Captain Brassbound's Conversion,
    27, 67, Notes to, 126, quoted,
    1–2, 48, 66, 67; *Devil's Disci-
    ple, The,* 27; *Heartbreak House,*
    27
Shelley, P. B., 115
Sherry, Prof. Norman, 26
Simón, Fray, 74
Smith, James Steel, 127
Smithers, Leonard, 45

Index   135

Social-Democrat, The, 34
Social-Democratic Federation, 19,
  20, 21
Socialist League, 19
Solomon, Simeon, 3
Spain, 26, 52, 82
Spanish-American War, 52
Speaker, The, 34; quoted, 57
Spectator, The, quoted, 57, 86
Spenser, Edmund: Faerie Queene,
  30
Spilsbury, Major A. G., 60
"Spy" (caricaturist), 29
Stallman, R. W., 127
Stead, W. T., 29
Stepniak, Sergei, (Kravchinsky,
  S. M.), 18, 29
Stevenson, Robert Louis:
  "Christmas at Sea", 30
Strang, William, 3, 27, 28
Swinburne, Algernon, 99; "Hymn
  to Proserpine", 30
Symons, Arthur, 29, 45, 116–17;
  quoted, 1, 45

Tarudant (Taroudant), 27, 59,
  60, 62
Tennyson, Alfred, Lord:
  In Memoriam, 72
Texas, 11, 14, 30, 31
Thorne, Will, 29
Tillett, Ben, 22, 29
Times, The, 21, 22; quoted, 40–
  41
Toft, Albert, 27, 29
Traherne, Thomas, 30
Transtextualities, 96–97

Tschiffely, A. F., 11, 16, 110,
  127
Turgenev, Ivan, 30, 58, 92
Twain, Mark, (Clemens, Samuel),
  30

Unwin, T. Fisher, 46
Urquiza, Justo José de, 9
Uruguay, 10, 93, 96

Valdivia, Pedro de, 69, 77–78
Verlaine, Paul, 30
Villon, François, 30
Voltaire (Arouet, F.-M.), 30, 57,
  115; Candide, 62, quoted, 70

Walker, John, 127
Wallace, Sir William, 7
Warren, Sir Charles, 20
Watts, Cedric (ed.), Joseph Con-
  rad's Letters to R. B. Cunning-
  hame Graham, quoted, 4, 29,
  38, 45, 59
Watts, Cedric, and Davies,
  Laurence, Cunninghame Graham,
  101
Wells, H. G., 3–4, 27, 29, 92;
  quoted, 4; When the Sleeper
  Wakes, quoted, 27–28
West, H. F., 110, 127; A Modern
  Conquistador, quoted, 38
Whistler, James M., 3, 28
Wilde, Oscar, 29, 46, 85; "Bal-
  lad of Reading Gaol, The", 30,
  85

Yeats, W. B., 116